RESPONSIBLE SCIENCE

OTHER NOBEL CONFERENCE BOOKS AVAILABLE FROM
HARPER & ROW

NOBEL CONFERENCE XXI

RESPONSIBLE SCIENCE
The Impact of Technology On Society

Merritt Roe Smith
Daniel J. Kevles
Salvador E. Luria
Winston J. Brill
J. Robert Nelson

Edited by
KEVIN B. BYRNE

1817

Harper & Row, Publishers, San Francisco

Cambridge, Hagerstown, New York, Philadelphia, Washington
London, Mexico City, São Paulo, Singapore, Sydney

FIRST EDITION

Library of Congress Cataloging-in-Publication Data

Nobel Conference (21st : 1985 : Gustavus Adolphus
   College)
   Responsible science.

   Papers presented at the 21st Nobel Conference
organized by and held at the Gustavus Adolphus College, St.
Peter, Minnesota, 1985.
   1. Technology—Social aspects—Congresses.
I. Smith, Merritt Roe,   . II. Byrne, Kevin B.
III. Gustavus Adolphus College.
T14.5.N58 1985   303.4'83   86-45013
ISBN 0-06-250128-3

---

86 87 88 89 90 HC 10 9 8 7 6 5 4 3 2 1

Contents

*To Benjamin,
and all future scientists*

Contributors

Merritt Roe Smith is professor of the history of technology at the Massachusetts Institute of Technology. He was a Harvard-Newcomen Fellow at Harvard University (1974–75), and has also received a number of awards, including an American Philosophical Society grant (1974); the Frederick Jackson Turner Award from the Organization of American Historians (1977); a Pulitzer Prize nomination (1977) and the Pfizer Award from the History of Science Society (1978) for *Harpers Ferry Armory and the New Technology;* and was an NSF scholar (1984). He is a member of the American Association for the Advancement of Science, the American Historical Association, the Organization of American Historians, the Society for the History of Technology, and the Society for Industrial Archeology. Smith is the author of *Harpers Ferry Armory and the New Technology: The Challenge of Change* (1977), *Military Enterprise and Technological Change: Perspectives on the American Experience* (1985), and numerous articles and reviews; he sits on the editorial board for Johns Hopkins Press, *Business History Review,* and *Technology and Culture.*

Daniel J. Kevles is professor of history at California Institute of Technology. Among the research grants he has won are a National Science Foundation Fellowship for Oxford University (1960–61); a Woodrow Wilson Fellowship (1961–62); an American Council of Learned Societies grant (1973); an NSF research grant (1978–80); an NEH Senior Fellowship (1981–82); and a Sloan Foundation research grant (1985–87). He was a member of the White House staff in Washington, D.C. (1964), and now belongs to the American Association for the Advancement of Science, Phi Beta Kappa, the Organization of American Historians, the History of Science Society (president of West Coast branch, 1978–80), the American Institute of Physics, and the British Society for the History of Science. Kevles is the author of *The Physicists: The History of a Scientific Community in*

Modern America (1978) and *In the Name of Eugenics: Genetics and the Uses of Human Heredity* (1985); he also serves as advisory editor of *Isis* and is a contributor to numerous academic journals, popular magazines, and newspapers.

Salvador E. Luria is director of the Center for Cancer Research and Sedgwick Professor of biology at the Massachusetts Institute of Technology. In 1969 he received the Nobel Prize in medicine. Luria was a research fellow at Curie Laboratory, Institute of Radium, Paris (1938–40), and a Guggenheim Fellow at Vanderbilt and Princeton universities (1942–43). He is a member of the American Academy of Arts and Sciences, the American Association for the Advancement of Science, the National Academy of Sciences, Sigma Xi, the American Society of Microbiology (president, 1967–68), the American Philosophical Society, and the American Society of Naturalists. He is the author of numerous papers and abstracts on bacteriology, microbial genetics, virology, and biological effects of radiation, and an editor or editorial board member of the *Journal of Bacteriology*, *Virology*, *Biological Abstracts*, the *Experimental Cell Research Journal*, and the *Journal of Molecular Biology*.

Winston J. Brill is vice president of research and development for Agracetus, a high-tech agricultural specialty firm located in Middleton, Wisconsin. He is also an adjunct professor in the department of bacteriology at the University of Wisconsin. Brill was a Henry Rutgers Fellow at Rutgers University (1961) and has earned numerous awards, including the Eli Lilly Award in Microbiology and Immunology (1979) and the Alexander von Humboldt Foundation Award (1979). He has served on the Genetic Engineering Advisory Panel to the U.S. Secretary of State (1981) and is currently a member of the USDA Policy Advisory Committee. He belongs to the American Association for the Advancement of Science and the American Society of Microbiology. Brill is the author of more than 125 publications on the genetics, molecular biology, biochemistry, and ecology of biological nitrogen fixation and is on the editorial board of the *Journal of Biotechnology*, *Trends in Biotechnology*, and *Critical Reviews in Biotechnology*.

J. Robert Nelson is director of the Institute of Religion, Texas

Medical Center, and clinical professor of community medicine, Baylor College of Medicine. Formerly, he was professor of systematic theology and dean of Boston University School of Theology. He has served as consultant to the President's Commission for Study of Ethical Problems in Medicine (1981–82). Nelson belongs to Phi Beta Kappa, the American Theological Society (president, 1975), the American Academy of Arts and Sciences, the American Association for the Advancement of Science, and the Hastings Institute for Ethics, Life Sciences, and Society. He was listed on the *Sports Illustrated* Silver Anniversary All-America football team. He is the author of *Criterion for the Church* (1963), *Doctrines of the Future* (1979), *Science and Our Troubled Conscience* (1980), *Human Life: A Biblical Perspective for Bioethics* (1984), and more than three hundred book chapters, essays, and book reviews. In addition, he serves as associate editor of the *Journal of Ethical Studies* and editor-at-large of *The Christian Century*.

Acknowledgments

The essays and discussions that comprise this book formed the basis of the twenty-first annual Nobel Conference, held at Gustavus Adolphus College on October 1 and 2, 1985. The conference provided two days of intellectual stimulation, which the present volume intends to sustain.

I had attended more than a dozen previous Nobel conferences, but had always viewed the action from the audience. Nobel XXI allowed me to see things from the other side of the podium, including the incredible process of planning and preparation that forms a significant part of the story for any gathering of such magnitude. Here, in only the briefest form, is that story.

Bill Heidcamp, of the biology department of Gustavus Adolphus College, initially noted the timeliness of a conference that would explore the social ramifications of advances in science, especially microbiology. President John Kendall of Gustavus subsequently suggested broadening that theme to explore the impact of science and technology on society. And so the topic for Nobel XXI was born.

Numerous people helped to translate the idea into reality. A committee of Gustavus faculty gave generously of their time and expertise. John Lammert, Richard Fuller, and John Bolkom deserve special mention. Drs. John Najarian and Murray Rosenberg of the University of Minnesota and Charles Denney of Minneapolis provided assistance, too, as did Professor Alex Roland of Duke University.

The support staff at the college, morever, performed superbly. Elaine Brostrom ran the show with grace and aplomb, and Dee Waldron, Becky Fritz, Jeanie Reese, and Janine Genelin provided secretarial assistance. Steve Waldhauser, Dennis Paschke, Dale Haack, and their respective crews handled a wide variety of necessary services most ably. For her organization of the closing banquet, Linda Fullerton receives our thanks.

Without yet others the conference could not be. The Nobel Foundation of Stockholm has allowed Gustavus Adolphus College to use the Nobel name. The GTE Foundation provided financial assistance for this particular conference. And to the Russell Lund family, whose generosity now permanently endows the conferences, the college offers its heartfelt gratitude.

Steve Dietz of Harper & Row was instrumental in the creation of this volume; for his patience and suggestions I extend my thanks. And to Richard Q. Elvee, the program director of the conferences, I owe my thanks for guidance, encouragement, and the opportunity to be a part of Nobel XXI.

Introduction

For more than two decades, the Nobel conferences have drawn large numbers of people to Gustavus Adolphus College in Saint Peter, Minnesota. While the crowds have grown in size, the general thrust of the two-day conferences has remained constant: to assemble a panel of experts to address a science-based theme. The audience has ranged from college and university professors to high school instructors and some of their students to interested citizens. At times the conference has focused on very specific issues; in contrast, the planners of Nobel Conference XXI intended that the conference explore a topic with vast implications—the impact of science and technology on society—in a way that could be understood by those most affected, the general public.

As one of those planners. I deemed it noteworthy when a member of the audience approached me after the final session of Nobel XXI. She spoke briefly, in words that I would have wanted to share with the five participants who had delivered their lectures and interacted with one another, both intellectually and socially, over the previous two days. "I have been to every Nobel Conference in the past twenty-one years," she announced, "and I want you to know that this was the clearest, most understandable one I have attended."

The opinion uttered by this seasoned participant from the audience was important to me. In her case, at any rate, the conference had succeeded in one of its chief aims. The lectures and discussions had without doubt considered many complex, important topics. To hear—even from a single observer—that the speakers had covered their subjects in a way comprehensible to the general public was especially gratifying.

Its planners also believed that the conference dealt with a timely subject. One decade earlier, for instance, certain scientific researchers had held a major conference at Asilomar, California, to examine the potential social impact of their efforts. They were microbiologists, and their research involved a technique called genetic engineering or gene splicing. Their intent was to evaluate the potential dangers of this young but quickly growing area of scientific endeavor. They confronted crucial questions, considering what, if any, restraints they ought to place on their own work. Concluding that the benefits outweighed the risks, they decided that their research ought to continue, although with a great deal of care. Yet, microbiology had clearly reached a point analogous to physics at the time of the Manhattan Project. Genetic engineering might prove to be Pandora's box, better left closed. But the fact was that the box was open. Given the importance of the issues at stake, it seemed appropriate now, ten years after that meeting of microbiologists, to reopen their inquiry. And more.

In that intervening decade not only microbiology had taken dramatic strides. Indeed, the technological application of science in general had made tremendous changes in society from the mid-1970s to the mid-1980s. Robotization in industry, computerization in many areas, lasers, the mechanical heart, genetically altered organisms, artificially produced hormones—these examples represent only the most visible and pervasive instances of recent technology that have significantly shaped the contours of society and social living. These are the results of heady and exhilarating science, to be sure. But while these examples represent magnificent science and technological application, one might well wonder what a careful examination of the social impact of these developments might show.

For if science has had tremendous ramifications upon society in a relatively short time, it is also true that technology has on occasion produced nightmare rather than nirvana. The word *Bhopal* has become synonymous with industrial, chemical catastrophe, recalling the mass death that resulted from a leak at the Union Carbide plant in Bhopal, India. *Love Canal* is a term loaded with ironic reference, designating as it does that body of polluted water in New York state that has called into question the fitness of a populated area for human (or perhaps for any) habitation. *Three Mile Island* calls to mind the limitations and dangers of nuclear power, referring to the releases of radioactivity and threatened meltdown at the nuclear power generator outside Harrisburg, Pennsylvania.

The individuals asked to address the audience at Nobel XXI were people who could shed light on the vast issues contemplated by the conference's planners. These participants had no ideological axes to grind against science and technology. Nobel laureate Salvador Luria, professor of biology and director of cancer research at Massachusetts Institute of Technology, agreed to share insights derived from a lifetime of work in science. A younger scientist, Winston Brill, accepted the invitation to represent another segment of the profession—scientists who have entered the commercial world. Brill is vice president of research and development for Agracetus, a firm specializing in the agricultural application of biotechnology. Two other speakers brought yet a third perspective to the conference. Merritt Roe Smith, professor of the history of technology at MIT, and Daniel Kevles, professor of history at California Institute of Technology, are individuals who see the present in the context of the past. They sought to place the issues in an appropriate historical context, each with reference to his specialty within the field of history. And J. Robert Nelson agreed to speak about ethical and theological dimensions of the topic, a viewpoint represented at each conference. As director of the Institute of Religion at Texas Medical Center, Dr. Nelson occupies a position that keeps him in close touch with the ethical issues that confront technology (especially medical technology) today. Each participant presented an address, then discussed the paper with the entire panel, and answered questions submitted by the audience. The final session brought all the panelists together to respond to questions put once again by members of the audience.

From panelists as obviously qualified and professionally varied as these credentials indicate, one might well have expected a provocative, informative conference. For their part, the conferees lived up to those expectations. As the proceedings developed, moreover, a major theme began to emerge: although science discovers, we are all to a greater or lesser degree involved with and affected by decisions of how to apply those discoveries. Questions of judgment and values permeate issues relating to the use of science-based technology. These issues are more complicated than merely choosing between "good" and "evil." They involve a societal decision as to what is good, or which of competing goods to pursue. These decisions may involve a choice between two or more paths, each of which leads to undesirable as well as desirable effects. Society and its leaders, then, make decisions that determine whether technology will be used responsibly or not, to which among many responsible uses the technology will be put, and what level of undesirable effect will be tolerated. These are matters that ultimately demand the attention of the entire society: business leaders, politicians, scientists, and citizens. The concept of responsibility thus emerged as a central theme as the speakers proceeded to assess the impact of science and technology on society. Hence the title of the present volume.

Merritt Roe Smith sounds this theme clearly in the first essay in this volume. In exploring "the promises and pitfalls of viewing technology as the primary vehicle of social progress," Smith's essay ranges from the days of the early American republic to the present, considering the continuities and changes in the societal perception of technology and progress. Thomas Jefferson, for instance, saw technology as progressive, but only as a means to a greater end—that of general human betterment, not simply in material terms but in spiritual, intellectual, and moral terms as well. In Jefferson's time, his vision was influential. But over the years the societal view of progress changed, growing less personal in its goals as industrial technology altered America in the mid-nineteenth century. Ralph Waldo Emerson captured the tension of a society fascinated with the products of this emerging technological progress but personally fearful of the competition to labor that machines presented. Reactions to the term *progress* had become deeply ambivalent, not only among groups of people but even for the same person.

Smith argues that this separation of human concerns from the concept of progress has led to a central dilemma for today's society. Taking the automobile industry as an example, Smith observes that automakers from Henry Ford down to the present have emphasized technology at the expense of human values. One result has been high profits. Another has been worker dissatisfaction in spite of the industry's relatively high pay scale.

By failing to consider individual human needs—as Jefferson might have done—American industry has generated considerable unrest even as it has produced material betterment. The American public, Smith concludes, is still ambivalent about technology and its relation to progress. To deal with matters responsibly, society must recognize the need to confront hard questions about technological progress: what kind of progress does society wish, and what price is it willing to pay for it?

The emphasis in Daniel Kevles's essay, on the other hand, presents a different historical consideration, less concerned with the economy and more directed toward the history of an intellectual, ethical issue. In an entertaining yet serious exploration of the past, Kevles considers the conflict between scientific knowledge and religious authority. He focuses on the relationship between eugenics—the improving of the human race through "scientifically" controlled breeding—and religion. Francis Galton, the Englishman who began the eugenics movement in the late nineteenth century, fully expected his idea to become a secular religion. Initially, it did provoke clerics. By the 1920s, however, modern-thinking Protestant clergy deemed eugenics theory acceptable, at least in part because, as Kevles explains, the targets of eugenics programs to restrict the procreation of certain "undesirable" elements in the population did not include the congregants of these clergy.

Kevles is particularly aware of the currency of this issue. He refers, for example, to a resolution signed in 1983 by distinguished clergy calling for a halt to certain genetic research. That resolution made manifest a "broad clerical consensus against attempts genetically to engineer new human beings." Explaining why he believes a conflict between science and religious authority has arisen again, Kevles concludes that society ought to welcome clerical involvement in scientific questions, assuming it is informed by considerable technical knowledge. When such involvement is not grounded in that knowledge, he implies, clerics—and society in general—might find themselves supporting bogus theories such as eugenics.

For his part, Salvador Luria is also concerned about knowledge and understanding. Luria, Nobel laureate in medicine, has long argued that scientists (and all human beings) must come to grips with the social and political implications of what they do. He believes passionately that scientists must commit themselves to social as well as professional goals. His essay shares this theme of personal commitment with some of the world's great literature. Fittingly, Luria's paper ranges across philosophy, literature, and history, as well as science. He argues that scientists *must* recognize that although their work is in itself value free, "the very existence of science is the product of a human society permeated with values—in fact, contradictory sets of values."

Borrowing the title for his essay from a poem by Wallace Stevens, Luria asserts that human beings derive meaning in their lives through participation in collective human enterprise. Scientists are not excepted; their lives are meaningful in part because they engage in the collective enterprise called science. But science does not exist in a vacuum, either historical (as Smith and Kevles have shown) or political. Science is the basis for technology, and technology in turn is the basis of our society, "a human society permeated with values." Scientists thus have a responsibility that transcends the doing of science, that demands participation in the society outside of the laboratory. Through participation in this collective human enterprise—the political realm—scientists add to the meaning in their lives. The object is not to politicize science. Rather, it is to recognize that scientists cannot ignore the social consequences of their science and resultant technology. They must enter the world of values, all the more crucial because "contradictory sets of values" exist in society. A deep sense of commitment to the scientific *and* the political, Luria ardently believes, is important if the scientist is to live a meaningful life.

Like Salvador Luria, Winston Brill has been an academic microbiologist—until recently, that is. Brill has joined a growing number of biotechnological researchers who have left the world of the university to move into a world where science and business intersect. His paper describes some of the exciting developments currently happening in commercial genetic engineering, especially those that apply to agriculture. It also examines and answers criticisms raised against that technology.

Brill is understandably optimistic about genetic engineering, a technology that has become increasingly widespread and simpler to do. Humankind, he points out, has interfered in the processes of nature for many years—for instance, through selective breeding and control of nutrition for animals. The meat we eat, the flowers we buy, the houseplants we have around us are all the products of human intervention. Genetic engineering is simply another step—albeit an exhilarating one—in that direction. In a few years it has already produced important products (especially in health care) and it promises to deliver much more. Rather than adding to our problems by unleashing new "superweeds" or deadly microorganisms upon the world, researchers in agricultural gene splicing are seeking ways to minimize or eliminate the problems that now threaten our environment and our health. A case in point is that of chemical fertilizer, a widespread water pollutant. Brill notes that if genetic engineers are successful, they will produce plants that need much less fertilizer than currently used. Recognizing that these issues are subject to political discussion, Brill echoes Professor Luria in calling for open, informed, and rational discussion among knowledgeable parties. He, too, believes that rational argument will prevail in the marketplace of ideas, if that marketplace is truly free. For, as he concludes, we will see that our new technology of gene splicing is really a move "back to nature."

J. Robert Nelson's paper rounds out the presentations in fitting style. His essay ranges widely, exploring the worlds of microbiology, medical technology, and computers. The alliterative title is a clue to the thrust of the paper: it investigates the implications of two opposing world views, that of the mechanistic materialist and that of the thoroughgoing spiritualist. Although adhering to neither of these philosophies, Nelson is especially concerned with the former, as it appears to be a dominant ethos in our technologically oriented culture.

Nelson suggests that none but a few of us would want to renounce the achievements of technology. Yet, he is anxious, expressing his concern about what he calls the "pathological consequences" of technology with respect to four areas: genetic research, engineered reproduction, the artificial heart, and computers. His fear is that in the drive to apply science to society—which is essentially what technology does—human beings will forget human values. Recombinant DNA may be the cutting edge of genetic science, for example, but humanity loses if that technology devolves into eugenics or disrupts ecosystems. Computer technology may provide humankind with a marvelously efficient machine, but what of the effect on the human pysche and economic system if the result is push-button labor or massive unemployment? Mechanical hearts, mechanical intelligence, and scientifically assisted reproduction may have distinct benefits to society, but they cannot exist at the expense of that which is human. In Nelson's judgment, scientists must constantly reaffirm the importance of the integrated individual, body and soul together.

These are the principal thrusts of the papers. Areas of agreement are obvious, but areas of disagreement exist, too. The discussion that followed each presentation at the conference, and the general panel discussion (which was the last session of the conference) provided the participants with the opportunity to question, to disagree with, to amplify upon, or to support the observations and interpretations put forth by one another. These sessions allowed for wider participation, too, as panelists answered questions from the audience. The discussions appear in edited form in this volume.

Clearly, the participants addressed themes crucially important to people living in an age more influenced by science and technology than most of us can imagine. And, if the woman who spoke to me at the close of the conference is at all typical, they did so in a manner accessible to a generally informed public. In the spirit of sharing their insights with a broad audience, and of continuing the conversations begun by their provocative papers, these proceedings are put before the reader.

1. Technology, Industrialization, and the Idea of Progress in America

MERRITT ROE SMITH

"Science finds—industry applies—man conforms."[1] Though little noticed at the time, these bold words epitomized the main theme of Chicago's Century of Progress International Exposition in 1933. Everywhere—in artwork, architecture, exhibits, lighting, and overall symbolism—the fair's promoters underscored the idea that progress rests on technology. Reflecting on the same theme in a book written to commemorate the Chicago fair, historian Charles A. Beard observed that "technology is the fundamental basis of modern civilization," "the supreme instrument of modern progress." "Of all the ideas pertinent to the concept of progress," he emphasized, "none is more relevant than technology."[2]

But that was more than fifty years ago. In view of recent events like the accidents at Bhopal, Love Canal, and Three Mile Island, as well as the continuing nuclear arms race, today's audience is likely to consider such pronouncements overstated, even naive. Have public attitudes changed or does the Promethean ethos manifest at Chicago continue to hold sway in our society? How have Americans viewed technology historically? What popular technological legacies live on in the American mind and how have these experiences shaped our present perceptions of technological change? What is the relationship between technology and the idea of progress in America? Obviously,

I wish to thank Leo Marx, Michael Smith, Sarah Deutsch, and Lindy Biggs for reading and commenting on an earlier draft of this paper. Their recommendations were invaluable.

these questions have no easy answers. This essay addresses the promises and pitfalls of viewing technology as the primary vehicle of social progress.

CHANGING PERCEPTIONS OF PROGRESS: THE EROSION OF THE JEFFERSONIAN VIEW

The idea of progress is deeply rooted in American culture. Briefly defined, it consists of the belief that things are getting better and better and that eventually the good life will be achieved "across the entire range of human endeavor" primarily through advances in science and technology.[3] Although the concept can be traced back to classical times, its modern phase dates to the seventeenth century (the age of the Scientific Revolution) and is associated with thinkers like Sir Francis Bacon and René Descartes. In its American form, the idea of progress initially drew more vitality from evangelical religion and the frontier experience than from science or technology, though that relationship changed appreciably as the United States achieved independence and entered a period of sustained economic growth. That the frontier experience fostered an aggressive "go-ahead" mentality among Americans while evangelical Protestantism encouraged a strain of millennial optimism that melded nicely with earlier Calvinistic beliefs about individual predestination and national destiny is often remarked. Clearly, the idea of progress and the idea of destiny are closely intertwined in American history.[4] Together they form our culture's dominant conception of history—much of which is mythological, to be sure, but which nonetheless permeates our perspective both as individuals and as a nation. The quasi-religious character of the idea of progress needs to be underscored in this context because it helps us to understand why the concept is so deeply rooted in American culture and why, as Leo Marx so aptly puts it, "a causal nexus exists between progress *within* science and technology and the general progress of humanity."[5]

What constitutes progress? Intellectual, material, moral, political improvement? Given the definition just provided, these categories seem adequate. However, complications arise because meanings shift and emphases vary over time. What we mean by progress today is markedly different from what was meant in the eighteenth century. Take, for example, Thomas Jefferson's views about the subject. No one of his generation held science and technology in greater esteem. Yet, as much as he revered discovery and invention, he always kept them in perspective and considered them *means* to achieving a larger social end. For Jefferson, progress ultimately meant the realization of a republican polity (with its emphases on liberty and virtue) in a predominantly agrarian society. "The manners and spirit of a people" counted most to him because they helped to "preserve a republic in vigour." As for factory cities and large-scale manufacturing enterprises, he feared that their unconstrained growth would eat like a cancer into the social fabric and destroy the laws and constitution of the United States. "Let our workshops remain in Europe," he admonished in 1787. "While we have land to labour then, let us never wish to see our citizens occupied at a workbench, or twirling a distaff."[6]

Although Jefferson held these views throughout his life, his actions as president and public policy maker ironically helped launch the United States into the Industrial Revolution. To him credit is due, for example, for first calling attention to interchangeable manufacturing methods in European armories and urging their adoption in the United States— a development that subsequently became one of the primary sources of mass production in America. Later in life, he even admitted in correspondence with friends the need for a factory system of production.[7] What deserves special emphasis here is that his reservations about large-scale manufacturing reflected a more general concern about the implications of progress. Like many of his compatriots, Jefferson worried that progress in some areas could mean backsliding in others. As one of the primary architects of the American governmental system, he well recognized how precarious the equilibrium between liberty, power, and virtue really was and how easily republics could be corrupted. In the minds of late eighteenth-century Americans, thin lines separated virtue from vice, prosperity from decadence, and civilization from savagery. If carried to extremes, the civilizing process of technology and industrialization could easily be corrupted and bring down the moral and political economy he and his contemporaries had worked so hard to erect. Given the seriousness of this threat, Jeffersonians (as well as many other Americans) could never completely shed their misgivings about the factory system, even though they allowed it and, in many cases, actively participated in it. When they spoke of progress, as they often did, they consequently gave human betterment (intellectual, moral, spiritual) equal weight with material prosperity. Without betterment, prosperity was meaningless. The pursuit of science and the development of technology doubtless occupied an important place in this scheme of things. But as means to larger social ends, they assumed a lesser order of magnitude in the Jeffersonian scale of values.[8]

When Thomas Jefferson died in 1826, the United States had already joined the Industrial Revolution. By that time, the Boston Manufacturing Company's famous "integrated" textile mill at Waltham, Massachusetts, had been in operation well over a decade and scores of mechanized factories dotted the eastern landscape of America. In the same year, a little-known Yankee mechanic named John H. Hall unveiled a complete set of wood- and metal-working machinery capable of manufacturing firearms with interchangeable parts and actually demonstrated the practicality of the concept before an astonished group of government officials. Only a year earlier, the Erie Canal had successfully linked the Great Lakes with the Hudson River, thus opening an enormous hinterland market to New York City and inaugurating a transportation revolution that would culminate decades later with the completion of a transcontinental railroad system.[9] Clearly, a new era had dawned and with it emerged a different set of attitudes about progress in general and the role technology would play in it. Slowly but perceptibly, the belief in progress began to shift away from the moral and spiritual anchors of the revolutionary era toward a more utilitarian and hardheaded business-oriented emphasis on profit, order, and prosperity.[10]

Specifying exactly when and where these new attitudes first appeared is difficult. No doubt they had resided in the culture all along, only to become more manifest as the pace of technological change quickened during the early national period (c. 1787–1825). In any case, one finds ample evidence of the new viewpoint among Jefferson's contemporaries, particularly those merchants and politicians who supported Alexander Hamilton's controversial programs for national economic development during the 1790s.

A case in point is Tench Coxe (1755–1824). A prickly Philadelphia aristocrat who eventually ended up as a middle-level civil servant (Purveyor of Public Supplies), Coxe emerged as the new nation's foremost political economist and exponent of industrial development during the years that spanned the administrations of five presidents from the 1780s to the 1820s. Like many of his contemporaries, he believed that America's political independence hinged on the establishment of economic independence. Given the country's lowly economic status, he emphasized the need for machine-based manufactures as the prime solution to its political problems. Indeed, he told an audience of sympathetic listeners in the summer of 1787 that manufacturing represented "the means of our POLITICAL SALVATION."

It will consume our native productions . . . it will improve our agriculture . . . it will accelerate the improvement of our internal navigation . . . it will lead us once more into the paths of virtue by restoring frugality and industry, those potent antidotes to the vices of mankind and will give us real independence by rescuing us from the tyranny of foreign fashions, and the destructive torrent of luxury.[11]

Contrary to those who viewed manufacturing as a threat to America's agrarian way of life. Coxe (a Jeffersonian in politics) held that mechanized industry would stimulate agriculture by consuming its products and creating even larger markets for agricultural goods. Throughout his writings, he tactfully subordinated manufactures to agriculture, referring to the latter as America's "great leading interest." Yet Coxe's priorities clearly contrast with Jefferson's. For Jefferson, progress meant the pursuit of science and technology in the interest of spiritual and material needs of people, and maintaining a proper balance between them. For Coxe, the emphasis shifted away from individual human needs to more impersonal societal ends, particularly the establishment of law and order. Coxe's anxiety about the nation's shaky economy clearly reflected an even deeper concern about the state of society. In his papers and addresses of the period, he repeatedly expressed his fear that "extreme poverty and idleness in the citizens of a free government will ever produce vicious habits and disobedience to the laws, and must render the people fit instruments for the dangerous purposes of ambitious men."[12] Convinced that such behavior would ultimately destroy the country's liberty, he thus supported the establishment of a strong central government as well as policy measures aimed at shoring up the republic against the excesses of democracy. In effect, he sought to substitute institutional for ideological constraints.

One measure, surely the one dearest to his heart, aimed at putting people to work in factories. "A man oppressed by extreme want is prepared for all evil and the idler is ever prone to wickedness," Coxe declared, "while the habits of industry, filling the mind with honest thoughts . . . do not leave leisure for meditating or executing mischief." The factory promised to employ the poor and indigent (particularly women and children) and "deliver them from the curse of idleness."[13] In a word, it would be more than a place of employment; it would be a moral gymnasium where "correct habits" of discipline, hard work, obedience, and punctuality could be inculcated. Every establishment of any size had work rules that enjoined employees from drinking, gambling, swearing, and loitering during working hours and prodded them to attend church on Sunday as well. But in the process of fostering a tightly controlled, paternalistic environment, factory masters established a wall between themselves and their employees that eventually led to bitter confrontations over wages, working hours, and general control over the shop floor. As industrialization proceeded apace, class distinctions became more pronounced as the face-to-face relationships of the traditional craft shop gave way to the bureaucratized rule of the factory. By the 1830s, considerable tension seethed beneath the surface of industrial achievement. What had begun as an honest effort to improve and stabilize society ended up fraught with ideological and class differences.[14]

In the midst of this strife, popular orators and journalists hailed "the progress of the age," reassuring their audiences that technological innovation not only exemplified but actually guaranteed progress. The evidence seemed incontrovertible. Decade by decade the pace of technological change quickened—railroads, steamships, machine tools, telegraphy, structures of iron and steel, electricity—and with each decade popular enthusiasm grew for inventors—these "Men of Progress"—and their inventions. Owing to their efforts, Ralph Waldo Emerson exclaimed, "life seems almost made over new." "Are not our inventors," asked another enthusiastic writer, "absolutely ushering in the very dawn of the millennium?" It certainly seemed so to Horace Greeley, the editor of the *New York Tribune*. Upon visiting that city's Crystal Palace Exhibition in 1853, he pronounced: "We have universalized all the beautiful and glorious results of industry and skill. We have made them a common possession of the people. . . . We have democratized the means and appliances of a higher life." In Greeley's opinion, technology had become democracy's greatest ally.[15]

Not everyone saw things the same way, however. Members of America's intellectual community—artists such as Thomas Cole; writers such as Nathaniel Hawthorne, Herman Melville, and Henry David Thoreau—expressed serious misgivings about the new technology and its social consequences. One thinks, for example, of Hawthorne's ingenious short story, "The Celestial Railroad" (1843), in which the steam locomotive and its cars are depicted as a satanic implement following a path straight to hell. Others, such as Emerson, felt more ambivalent about the changes taking place, at times hailing the "mechanic arts" as a great liberating force for humanity and on other occasions expressing concern about their implications. The sage of Concord seemed to grow more pessimistic with the passage of time. "What have these arts done for the character, for the worth of mankind?" he asked an audience in 1857. "Are men better?" The answer, unfortunately, seemed clear to Emerson. " 'Tis too plain," he concluded, "that with the material power the moral progress has not kept pace. It appears that we have not made a judicious investment. Works and days were offered us, and we took works."[16]

Emerson came closer than perhaps any other writer of his time to capturing the tensions that confronted working people in nineteenth-century America. Reflecting the powerful influence Protestant theology and republican ideology exercised on the popular imagination, this tension consisted of a bifurcated view of industrial progress. On the one hand, workers (like other Americans) were fascinated with the age's technical creativity as well as the ingenious products that issued from it. On the other hand, they frequently became apprehensive when new techniques actually entered their workplaces and threatened to upset and rearrange accustomed methods of doing things. No one knows whether large numbers of workers actually read Emerson's writings about technology, let alone appreciated his complex double-edged message. I suspect they did not. Emerson the philosopher and the common factory hand lived in different social worlds and operated on different planes of perception and understanding. Emerson sought to extrapolate to the highest level of human experience; workers had to cope with their own immediate experiences. While Emerson blamed the "mechanic arts" for the country's materialistic emphases and threatened spiritual bankruptcy, workers worried about more mundane issues such as the design, deployment, and management of new machines and the effect they might have on wages, hours, and working conditions.

American working people seem to have been ambivalent about innovations that impinged on their work ways. While they seldom completely repudiated the new technology, they did not fully embrace it either. Instead they vacillated between the old and the new, curious—even admiring—but always apprehensive. As citizens and consumers, however, their attitude toward technology often took a different twist. Here, owing partly to patriotic pride and partly to personal predispositions, working-class Americans seemed to embrace the idea of progress as fervently as members of other classes. This is amply attested to by their eager acquisition of industrial products, their admiration of others, and their strong support for public education. Without question, one's view of progress depended, among other things, on whether one was at home or at work, at the store or in the mill. Recognizing the existence of this double-sided attitude toward technology helps us grasp more clearly the complexities as well as the paradoxes inherent in the idea of progress and how perceptions of it varied among different segments of the population. Progress not only meant different things to different social classes, but also different things to the same person.[17]

Was Emerson correct? Had the country—its people and its institutions—sacrificed moral progress for material power? Had the critical balance between spiritual growth and worldly prosperity, a concern so central to Americans of Jefferson's era, been lost? The answer, I believe, is yes, although some qualification is needed. With rapid industrial growth, the population gradually drifted away from its revolutionary republican moorings toward a more secular and materialistic frame of belief. It did so more by default than by conscious choice. To be sure, the old republican creed could still be heard occasionally in Fourth of July speeches and on other celebratory occasions, but its purpose was primarily rhetorical, its effect nostalgic. In its place had emerged a new creed that glorified the "march of invention" and the material "progress of the age."[18] Henry Adams, one of the most astute observers of nineteenth-century America, witnessed these changes and wrote movingly about them in his famous autobiography. At the outset, he recognized the impact technology had exerted on his life through railroads, steamboats, and telegraphy. But the capstone came when he attended the Paris Exposition of 1900 and witnessed the tremendous invisible power generated by electric dynamos. Awed by the experience, Adams reported that he "began to feel the forty-foot dynamos as a moral force, much as the early Christians felt the Cross." Moreover, he sensed that the dynamo had replaced the cross as the primary force in civilization. Indeed, he found himself praying to it! For Adams, the contrast between the dynamo and the cross symbolized an enormous shift of faith away from the great principles of Christianity toward those of science and utility. The former stood for love; the latter for power. For Adams, as for Emerson, the contrast between these two "kingdoms of force" spoke volumes about what had been lost through industrialization. Nearly forty years earlier, in 1862, Adams had observed to his brother Charles that "man has mounted science and is now run away with." By 1900, the truth of that statement seemed even clearer.[19]

In summary, this brief reconnaissance into the nineteenth century has revealed that, prior to the Civil War, Americans turned away from an essential part of the republican ethos and, in doing so, lost touch with basic human and moral sentiments that had originally informed the idea of progress. Bolstered by a seemingly endless stream of triumphs in science and technology, social leaders became increasingly arrogant about what could be achieved through rationalization and standardization and began to discount—even disparage—other beliefs that accentuated ambiguity and variability in human affairs. With the spiritual element effectively removed from the idea of progress, its materialistic aspects became dominant. The old parity between moral and material progress disappeared and with it emerged one of the central dilemmas of our present age, namely, an unbridled enthusiasm for technological innovation and the ascendancy of profit over tradition in the rush to rationalize all aspects of industrial life.

TECHNOLOGY AS PROGRESS: THE CASE OF THE AUTO INDUSTRY

Our attachment to the idea of progress in its modern utilitarian form has often caused us to overlook the human and environmental implications of technological change. This is not the place to present a comprehensive review of the shortfalls of progress. Suffice it to say that the evidence of such is plentiful.[20] Instead, let us look briefly at the automobile industry, an area of enterprise that became emblematic of American technological leadership in the twentieth century. This example will allow us to discern how progress as an idea is related to progress as an actual social process.

Of all the consequential innovations introduced during the twentieth century, the self-propelled motor vehicle stands at the top of the list. As in the case of virtually all new technologies, the introduction of the automobile had a number of unintended consequences. On the positive side, it extended one's freedom of choice, power, and mobility in ways that had never been dreamed of. On the other hand, its widespread use led to serious traffic problems (congestion, unsafe driving, and so on) and environmental problems (noise, air pollution) and, according to some observers, bore responsibility for increased sexual promiscuity, decreased church attendance, and the breakdown of family and neighborhood solidarity.[21] All these factors are sufficient to warn us of the ambiguities and doubts that complicate popular perceptions of the idea of progress. For the moment, however, I want to single out a more subtle problem, indigenous to industrialization, that initially affected a relatively small segment of the population but has had significant long-term consequences for everyone. I refer to mass production and the standardization of work.

The person who popularized the concept of mass production, of course, was Henry Ford. Between 1908 and 1914, his company introduced the famous Model T and developed manufacturing methods that completely transformed the automobile industry and rapidly diffused throughout the American and world technological communities. From the outset, Ford's disarming candor and hardheaded practicality captivated Americans. No doubt people saw a bit of themselves in the Flivver King, and they evidently liked what they saw. Tough, reliable, practical, and, above all, economical, the car aptly reflected Henry Ford's character.

With the resounding success of the Model T (fifteen million were made between 1908 and 1927), Ford assumed the mantle of a national folk hero. His opinion was sought on everything from politics to religion, and he seemed to have ready answers for just about everything. When asked, for example, what he thought about the debilitating environment of the city, he retorted curtly, "We shall solve the city problem by leaving the city."[22] Ford's pronouncements always seemed so disarmingly candid and simple, but embedded in them were deeply imbued values and attitudes that reflected the rural Protestant culture from which he came.

To be sure, Ford was a man with a mission. "I am going to democratize the automobile," he told a friend in 1909. "When I'm through, everybody will be able to afford one, and about everyone will have one." However, when it actually came to building Model Ts, Ford's "mass production for the people" took a singularly perverse turn away from democratic values toward autocracy. Ford the factory master and Ford the popular hero turned out to be quite different persons. While he enthusiastically promoted his "car for the great multitude," he adamantly rejected the notion of socioeconomic equality. "Most certainly all men are not equal," he wrote in his autobiography (1922), "and any democratic conception which strives to make men equal is only an effort to block progress." In Ford's utilitarian mind, democracy was inherently wasteful, and there was nothing he detested more than waste. Thus, even though he viewed himself as a benefactor of humanity—a businessman who worked not just for personal profit but also for social welfare—he adopted a quasi-military approach to production and steadfastly refused to acknowledge the equality of people on the shop floor with himself. In Ford's hierarchical world (as in Huxley's *Brave New World*), everything had its assigned place. Hired labor's place was to stand at command and submit to the rules of the employer.[23]

Ford's manufacturing approach, popularly known as Fordism, emphasized principles of efficiency, rationality, continuity, and speed. Specifically, it consisted of a highly integrated and closely managed system of single-purpose machine tools, standardized fixtures and gauges, moving assembly lines, and absolute interchangeability of parts. The key words here are *system* and *rationality*. Compared with earlier industrial methods, what is noteworthy about Ford's system is the degree to which it subordinated workers to machines. Prior to the advent of mass production, workers had pretty much controlled the pace of their work by virtue of their monopolization of essential skills. Under Fordism, this changed. Ford and his engineer associates—men like "Cast Iron" Charlie Sorenson and Pete Martin—made no bones about their desire to simplify individual work tasks and, if possible, replace skilled workers with machinery. Such thinking had long been a central premise of industrial engineers. But Ford was the first to carry it out on a massive scale. The idea was to simplify individual work assignments so that they could be performed by virtually anyone with a few days of training. In doing so, the Ford management team eliminated the need for large numbers of skilled molders and machinists, often the most independent and intractable of factory employees. Their places would be filled by "deskilled specialists" or machine tenders, all of whom performed basically the same tasks of inserting a workpiece in a preset machine, throwing a switch, and removing it. Such work, which reached its logical extreme on the assembly line, was highly repetitive and routinized with no opportunity for employees to exercise individual judgment. Fordism demanded a new degree of conformity. Instead of setting their own pace, workers found themselves being paced by the machine.[24]

The response to Ford's methods was predictable. Workers complained about the relentless pressure and deadly monotony of the assembly line and likened the company's new Highland Park factory to a lunatic asylum. Indeed, the comic episode in the movie *Modern Times* (1936) in which Charlie Chaplin's Little Tramp goes berserk after experiencing the speed and pressure of work on an assembly line was inspired by Chaplin's visit to Ford's Highland Park plant in 1923.[25]

Serious labor problems clearly existed at Highland Park. In 1913, the year Ford introduced the assembly line, daily absentee rates averaged around 10 percent of the total work force, while labor turnover reached an amazing 370 percent. This meant that on any given day from 1300 to 1400 workers stayed home and that "Ford managers had to hire more than 52,000 workers to maintain a workforce of about 13,600 persons." Needless to say, such problems seriously jeopardized the efficiency of Ford's operations.[26]

The company's solution was to institute the famous five-dollar day in January, 1914, an action that signaled an important trade-off in labor-management relations. In return for higher wages and shorter hours, Ford's employees submitted to a highly paternalistic welfare plan that imposed rigid controls on both their home life and their work day. In addition to condemning idleness as a disgrace and exalting the gospel of hard work, members of Ford's "Sociological Department" (his personnel office) actually entered the homes of workers, questioned them about personal affairs, and instructed them in such matters as personal hygiene, social behavior, and especially thriftiness. The company had a very definite idea of what thrift entailed. "By this," a company official stated in January 1914, "we mean that the employee shall not be addicted to the excessive use of liquor, nor gamble, nor engage in any malicious practice derogatory to good physical manhood or moral character." Moreover, he added, every Ford employee was expected to "conserve his resources and make the most of his opportunities that are afforded him in his work." Thrift thus had important moral connotations, but mainly it aimed at ensuring that employees would come to the plant fully prepared to work attentively and to give their best to the company.[27]

In the short run, money talked and Ford's paternalistic program got results. Within the space of a year, labor turnover fell from the phenomenally high levels of 1913 to 54 percent. During the same period, absenteeism decreased from 10 to around 2.5 percent. But in the long run, the program of social control failed. High wages simply could not compensate for the absence of humane working conditions. Although the Ford Motor Company paid the highest wages in the automobile industry, workers found the system oppressive. Labor turnover continued to be high because thousands of people simply could not stand the unrelenting pace and its accompanying pressures. Those who stayed on the job quickly learned how to slow the machine down through various forms of sabotage and subterfuge. Such practices allowed them to cope with their labor rather than take satisfaction from it. Although the trade-off between labor and management continued, it operated to neither side's satisfaction. Managers complained about labor's lack of commitment and loyalty to the firm while labor complained about harsh working conditions and a fundamental lack of respect on the part of their employers. At best, the high wage–hard work trade-off was a tenuous accommodation.[28]

Recent events in the auto industry reveal that the same old problems persist. Numerous investigators have documented the dissatisfaction that exists among workers, even though their wages and benefits remain among the highest in the land. Writing about the "Blue-Collar Blues" in the 1970s, for example, journalist Judson Gooding observed that "high absenteeism and quit rates, excessive rework and scrap, deliberate acts of soilage and vandalism, hostile resistance to supervision, and an increased willingness to strike" pervaded the work force. Other writers have detected the same symptoms while attributing them to deep-seated psychological and social problems inherent in mass production. Almost everyone agrees that high wages and excellent benefits have not generated the incentive, loyalty, and high quality work manufacturers initially expected. In this respect, money does not talk; the promise of material comfort has not produced widespread feelings of satisfaction and fulfillment. Indeed, by the 1970s, the high wage trade-off had become a distinct economic liability to manufacturers, especially after foreign competitors began to capture long-held American markets for mass-produced goods.[29]

Instead of directly confronting and resolving the social tensions inherent in mass production, industry leaders have tended to do what they have always done, namely, look for technological fixes. For them progress has meant designing the human element out of the production system. And, to a significant degree, they have succeeded. With critical support from military-funded research projects, large amounts of resources have been channeled into the development of automated production systems. The earliest of these, numerically controlled machine tools, appeared in the 1950s under Air Force sponsorship, although widespread applications of the new technology did not take place for nearly two decades. Today mass production industries, led by automakers, have moved well beyond specialized applications of automated machinery toward the deployment of highly integrated computer-controlled design and production systems for *entire* factories. The most noteworthy examples are computer-aided manufacturing (CAM) systems, computer-integrated manufacturing (CIM) systems, direct numerical control (DNC) systems, programmable controllers (PC), and, of course, robots like PUMA, General Motors's Programmable Universal Machine for Assembly. Collectively, these innovations and others like them form the core of what is now being called the Third Industrial Revolution.[30]

From a narrow economic perspective, the results are impressive. Even critics acknowledge the potential flexibility, productivity, and profitability of the new systems. Perhaps most important in the eyes of managers, computer-programmed machinery neither tires nor talks back. Like the mechanical slaves so often depicted in nineteenth-century American literature, they perform their tasks efficiently and without complaint. In this respect, the new technology presents an ideal solution to the perceived labor problem by solidifying management's control of the shop floor and lessening labor's influence. This is possible because managers now have direct access to computer programs that direct the machinery; they no longer have to rely as much on workers at the point of production. Having been designed to minimize the need for skills and to diminish the need for worker decision making, the new technology holds the promise of effectively establishing management's authority over labor.[31]

COMPUTER AUTOMATION: THE NEW TECHNOLOGICAL FIX

Presented with the prospect of cheaper goods of comparable, perhaps even better, quality, it is not surprising that most Americans (including working people) generally view computer automation as a positive force. That is, they see it as progress so long as it doesn't threaten their earning power or routinize and downgrade their labor. To say this, of course, is to acknowledge the paradoxical behavior Americans exhibit toward technological innovations. A machine operator may think nothing of buying a TV set made in an automated factory, but whether or not to bring a centrally controlled automatic production machine into his or her shop—that is a different question. Certain distinctions thus separate what people accept as progress and condemn as exploitation. The way people respond to change depends on what they do, how long they have been doing it, and where they stand in the organizational and social hierarchy. Questions of status, tradition, and control thus loom large in any discussion of technology and progress. By and large, American workers are no more antagonistic toward technological innovations than are other members of society. But when change threatens to undo certain valued rights and traditions, they quite naturally resist, as anyone would.

Unquestionably, automation, as currently practiced in the United States, poses a serious threat to working people. Even setting aside the hotly debated issues of deskilling, dislocation, and structural unemployment (all of which are attributed to automation), other reasons for concern exist. For one thing, workers consider employment in automated plants to be dead-end jobs with little or no chance for skill enhancement or advancement. At the same time, stress levels on the job remain as high as, or higher than, they were at Ford's Highland Park factory in the early 1900s. An even more ominous feature of the new technology is management's ability to monitor work more closely through various computer controls. Indeed, the technology has now advanced to the point that a supervisor can sit at a console with a CRT screen and keep track of scores of machines on a production line. Formerly, machine operators could pace themselves or take a break by putting in already finished work and, in effect, cutting air. Now by detecting the amount of electric power being used at each machine (power usage is higher when the machine is actually at work), supervisors can even tell when a machinist is goofing off. Employers no longer have to hire spies, as Henry Ford did, to tell them what is going on in the shop. Computer systems do it for them.[32]

Finally, the leverage mechanics used to exercise over their employers by virtue of their possession of special skills and knowledge of the shop floor is rapidly eroding. Given the tremendous flexibility and uniformity of the new computer technology, managers now can use it as a way of disciplining labor by threatening to move production to some other locality. This happened in 1973, for example, when General Motors, faced with a strike at its Cadillac Seville body plant in Detroit, moved the tapes containing all the information necessary to machine body dies to a nonstriking plant in Flint, Michigan. This is the ultimate advantage of automation to employers: it can be used to ward off and even break strikes. As the failure of the highly publicized Professional Air Traffic Controllers Organization (PATCO) strike in 1981 well illustrates, the advent of computerized automation has fundamentally altered "the balance of economic power in collective bargaining in management's favor."[33]

It might be argued that the internal problems of automated mass production touch a relatively small segment of the population and that, after all, far more people benefit from its products than are degraded by its processes. Should not the fears and grievances of working people be submerged in the interest of the larger good? To be sure, this position has some validity. Our society has achieved one of the highest standards of living in the world and we have already noted how Fordist methods helped to democratize the ownership of automobiles as well as all sorts of consumer products in America. *But* mass production has another dimension that is more problematic, namely, its authoritarian character and the larger effects it can have on a democratic society. Several writers—notably Lewis Mumford and Harley Shaiken—have pointed to the fundamental incompatibility that exists between authoritarian technics and democratic values. "When work is electronically demeaned in the office or the factory," Shaiken writes, "the repercussions carry far beyond the workplace." That "artifacts have politics" is unquestionable. As products of particular segments of society, technologies reflect the values of their creators and are thus loaded with ideological implications. How far dare we go before the authoritarian character of our leading technologies spills over and erodes our political and social system? Have we reached that point already?[34]

PROGRESS AND THE QUESTION OF PRIORITIES

How does all this bear upon the idea of progress in America? Should the belief in progress be jettisoned as a largely misguided dream? I think not. Although a number of intellectuals have predicted the idea's early demise in the twentieth century, it continues to exercise considerable sway among all segments of the population. At times, the belief in progress seems to recede in American culture (for example, 1930s, 1970s), only to reemerge evidently as strong as before. This remarkable resilience testifies to the doctrine's centrality in American culture. Indeed, it is so deeply rooted in the culture that I doubt if it could be extracted without our paying an unacceptably high psychological and economic price. I, for one, worry that we might sacrifice more by ridding ourselves of the concept than we would gain.

The idea of progress has its positive and negative aspects, to be sure. We have seen how appeals to progress have been used to condone profoundly antidemocratic practices in our society. We also have seen how modernization in the form of sophisticated, productivity-enhancing technologies and highly rationalized management controls are justified—often at the expense of working people—in the name of progress. But we also need to remind ourselves that, in its early formations, the idea of progress stood for high moral principles—more specifically, political liberty and a just society—and human betterment. In addition to fostering a "go-ahead"–"get-ahead" mentality among Americans, it aimed at strengthening our commitment to egalitarian as well as individual rights. Equally important, the belief in progress encourages hope: hope for the human race, hope for the improvement of its condition, hope that history will have a happy ending. These are perhaps heady dreams, but very commendable ones nonetheless.

Many years ago as an undergraduate, I read an article entitled "What Is Still Living in the Political Philosophy of Thomas Jefferson?" "In respect to particular forms and policies," the author concluded, much of Jefferson's philosophy was outmoded. But "in respect to fundamentals"—particularly the place of human rights and "the form of government best suited to secure them"—he found Jefferson's philosophy "still valid."[35] My message is that much is still living in the idea of progress in America. And not all of it is for the better. In our rush to pursue "sweet" problems, accumulate fortunes, and exercise power and influence, we have often substituted technocratic means for humanitarian ends and, in the process, lost sight of the priorities that people of Jefferson's day assigned to the idea of progress. To them progress meant material prosperity, to be sure. But it also meant growth of the human spirit and the abolition of inequalities in society.

That today's society is far more complex than that of Jefferson's era cannot be denied. Having discovered "that 'rationality' splinters our lives as rapidly as it orders them," we are far less sanguine about the inevitability of progress.[36] We have learned the hard way that not everyone profits from progress. We also have learned that technological progress does not necessarily mean social progress and that there are winners and losers in the process of technological change. The arms race, environmental deterioration, structural unemployment—all these press upon us ever harder. Faced with these dilemmas, perhaps it is time to get back to fundamentals. We need to rekindle the Jeffersonian ideal of the "middle landscape" with its sensitivity to the necessity for balance between the spiritual and material aspects of life, between nature and civilization. In the process, we have to be willing to ask, debate, repeat, and hope to resolve without recrimination or reprisal the hard questions: "Progress for whom? Progress for what? What kind of progress do we, as a society, really need?"[37]

PANEL DISCUSSION

KEVLES: It seems to me that your lecture raises an issue which is fundamental to the functioning of the American economy and to the quality of life in the United States. Do you have any thoughts on what sorts of trade-offs we can possibly make between the values of technological progress, economic competitiveness, and so on on the one hand, and humaneness in the work place on the other, given the fact that we are really no longer living in a domestic economy but in an international economy in which we have to worry about technological progress, competitiveness, etcetera, coming from abroad? A corollary to that is, for example, how do the Japanese do it?

SMITH: Well, it is a very interesting fact about early American history that there were certain choices made as early as 1800 about what shape the industrial system would take. The United States developed a style of technology and of industrialization that emphasized large scale, centralization, speed, and continuity which evolved into the mass production of today. The other option at that time was to have built an industrial system around more flexible technologies and smaller shops, smaller in the sense that they would have employed smaller work forces. A number of political economists, two of whom are colleagues of mine at MIT, today argue that what needs to be done with the development of these new computer-guided and -controlled devices and machine tools is to restructure the industrial base in a way that would make things more flexible and bring control down into a smaller shop framework than you see in mills that employ six, seven hundred or more workers. People like Michael Piore and Charles Sabel [of MIT] argue that by doing so you improve communications between owners and workers in fighting out battles over the question of shop floor control, which is obviously one of the key questions in all of these debates. These battles are less tense, they are less bitter than they are in the large-scale industrial style that we have today. So one possibility is to restructure industry; not to copy the Japanese, but really to restructure industry in a way that makes use of the flexibility that is brought to us by these new technologies.

KEVLES: Can you be as efficient and competitive, though, in small manufacturing environments?

SMITH: Part of the argument is yes, it would be as efficient. Again there is historical precedent for that. We know very well that the United States pioneered the development of interchangeable manufacturing with the mass production of firearms in the nineteenth century. We also know that in Great Britain that system was not developed, and yet British manufacturers were outproducing American manufacturers using handproduction techniques on this flexible scale. So there is plenty of evidence that going to a smaller scale doesn't necessarily lessen efficiency. That correlation, however, doesn't necessarily exist all of the time.

LURIA: May I add to that? It is not only a matter of scale. It seems to me that the absence of competition in American industry after the Second World War allowed for the maximizing of profits *and* wages. Unions and manufacturers more or less cooperated, then, in not worrying about the quality of the products, satisfying a certain market, or modernizing factories. When competition started again, coming especially from Japan, American industry was in that condition. It has really been a collaboration between the manufacturers and the workers to have high wages and rather old-fashioned manufacturing. So I'm not sure that the size of the operation is critical. The important thing is whether there is a true application of the most modern [technology], in order not only to maximize profits and wages in the short range but to create an American industry which is competitive and satisfactory. Certainly in the steel industry we are desperately in that condition, much more so than in auto.

NELSON: I have a sense of quandary and confusion over ways by which our country as a whole can realize its potential economically and technologically as well as culturally and in terms of basic human good. I'm concerned with the fact that we do not have generally in our country anymore a real sense of industrious responsibility. My concern is how it's possible without resorting to government regimentation or other kinds of restrictions upon human freedom to recover some of the sense of industriousness and of collective purpose that will restore craftsmanship and produce quality goods rather than the built-in obsolescence of much of our production, and also give us the better kind of social life that we are looking for. I just posed a great question. I think it is a massive problem before us in the United States. I'd like to know if Professor Smith has some thoughts on this issue.

SMITH: Again, when I look at the big picture of American history and I ask myself where the really creative acts of innovation and invention took place, the answer oftentimes is that they didn't happen in large-scale operations. They happened in small shops in which there was considerable interchange between workers, managers, and owners. The problems often arose once the new technologies were developed and began to be expanded and extrapolated on a much larger scale. That's when the problems began to appear. One of the most creative inventors of American machine tools in the nineteenth century was Simeon North, from Middletown, Connecticut. He had a shop of about sixty people. He is well known to have invented what is known as the plane milling machine, a basic machine tool. To my knowledge, North's shop never had a strike, never had any serious labor problems in the way that, say, a Lowell mill that employed six hundred did. It seems to me that the question of scale in that regard is important.

So much depends on who is running the shop and how they get along with people that they employ. It sounds so common-sensical, but it makes a difference. One of my research specialties is the history of industrial firms. Over and over again, people ask me why some communities entered the Industrial Revolution more easily than others. The answer oftentimes is that a lot depended on who was there managing the operations. The force of personality and the scale of operations within which that personality operates is very important. The idea that political economists are putting forward now about trying to restructure around smaller-scale operations and taking advantage of the new technologies is one that has possibilities. I think it's one that really ought to be considered and brought into this debate about "progress for what, progress for whom," because in doing so it gives workers a greater sense of participation in what's going on in the shop. That's very important.

KEVLES: You started your talk with our friend, Mr. Jefferson. It's true that Jefferson opposed industrialization, because he was afraid that it would lead to the alienation of the worker from his work, and also would take people away from the land and place them in cities where they would be propertyless. He said if people became piled high in cities, as in Europe, they would become corrupt, as they were in Europe. In short, the agrarian vision of Jefferson at its base was important to him because he believed that an agrarian society in which people worked their own land gave them a stake in their work and a stake in society, and therefore democracy could work because people would have a stake in stability.

What we have to do is to reinterpret Mr. Jefferson's very insightful perception about the relationship of people not only to their work, but also to the political and the social system in which they live. If people have a sense of a stake in their work and in their society, then they will be industrious and responsible toward it. If, however, they are alienated from it, they will be rebellious about it, and not care. The challenge that we face is one in which we can provide not only environments in which technological innovation will occur, but also work environments and social arrangements in which we can be confident that people will feel that they have a stake in their work and in their society. We should go back to Mr. Jefferson and recognize the fundamental human truth that he pointed to in his vision, and attempt to reinterpret it, however, for a contemporary, very complex industrial and technological society.

SMITH: That's well put. The only addendum I would make is that the culture of this country is unlike that of Japan. It would be a mistake for us to try to emulate the Japanese and think that we're going to regiment our work force like the Japanese work force is regimented, or seems to be regimented. The notion of individualism in this country is part of the problem. It's a very deeply held belief in our country. It is responsible for a lot of the country's creativity and dynamism, and it is responsible for a lot of the country's labor problems. It seems to me that any attempt on the part of a person who is confronted with trying to restructure the industrial system so that it moderates labor-management conflicts is going to have to be aware of the fact that the conflict never disappears. You moderate it, you try to reduce tensions as much as you can, but you'll never get one of these environments so antiseptic that there's not going to be some persons wanting to take a cigarette break at a certain point in the day when the boss doesn't want them to. That's not going to happen. It seems to me that when we talk about restructuring work, we have to remember that there are certain elements within this culture that are its strengths, and at the same time are its weaknesses. There are two sides to that story, in a way. When you look at the overall picture, the United States has been a very creative and dynamic industrial economy. It needs some tuning.

BYRNE: With the vast automation that's occurring in American industry, what is going to be the fate of the American workers? What recourse is left for the labor unions?

SMITH: The future for organized labor in this country doesn't look very good right now, especially in industries that are being automated. Look at these printer unions in New York and Washington and various strikes that they've faced in the last five years. They've been losers, and they're big losers. They have been drastically weakened in the sort of clout that they have against people who are introducing the automated systems. It varies from industry to industry, but now it looks as if the same thing is going to happen in the automobile industry. Certainly, leaders of the UAW are very well aware of the problems that they face and, in fact, one of the people I cited in my talk today, Harley Shaiken, has just written a book called *Work Transformed*. If you want to read a book that really talks about the issues that confront organized labor today and the serious condition that it's in, I would recommend that you take a look at that book.*

BYRNE: What about the displacement caused by the automation of industry?

SMITH: The thing that comes to mind is the famous interview that Edward R. Murrow had with Walter Reuther in the 1950s.

---

*Harley Shaiken, *Work Transformed: Automation and Labor in the Computer Age* (New York: Holt, Rinehart & Winston, 1985).

He said: "Mr. Reuther, what do you think of all this automation? It's really taking over jobs." Reuther looked at him and said, "Well, you know they're going to have to be people out there to buy those automobiles, and people have to have jobs in order to have the income to buy the automobiles." When you talk about displacement in society, it's a hard question to answer. They're going to go in a lot of different directions, I suspect.

KEVLES: Technological displacement has been going on for a long time. I don't know very well the history of what happened in the nineteenth century, but I do know something about the twentieth century. In the 1920s, there was enormous technological displacement from manufacturing industries, but there was also a growth of new industries fostered by technology; for example, radio and the automobile. There was at that time tremendous migration from the farms into the cities and the slack at that time seems to have been taken up by the growth of these new industries and also the creation of service industries that went along with them. For example, the automobile industry, even now, employs one out of seven people in the United States, not simply for manufacturing, but also for repair, for servicing, for gas stations, and so on, as well as all the supplier parts that are necessary for autombiles. In the last twenty-five to thirty years, as I understand it, there has been continuing displacement from production in the work force in manufacturing (that's one of the reasons that blue-collar labor unions are less powerful now than they used to be) into high tech industries and also into service industries. Again, what happened in the twenties has been repeated and continues to go on in the United States in the last twenty-five years or so. I don't see any reason why those service industries shouldn't continue to grow. And also at the same time why there shouldn't continue to be some kind of diminution in the minimum number of hours a week that everybody has to put in earning a living.

One of the interesting challenges that we face is not only the distribution of work, but how leisure will be employed. We know how it is being employed these days. There is growth in the entertainment industry, the sports industry, as well as the book industry, the movie industry, and the television industry, the VCR industry, etcetera, etcetera. How people want to use their time is up to them. Clearly, though, the creation of leisure creates a demand for economic functions that fill leisure. So, one can see these trends from manufacturing, to service, to entertainment, and so on. I suspect that they will continue. How each of us chooses to take advantage of them, however, is a question of how each of us chooses his or her own destiny.

SMITH: I said in the talk that there are winners and losers in technological change. Part of the meaning of that expression is that when change comes, people will be displaced. It has happened; it happened one hundred fifty years ago; it is happening now; it will continue to happen. One of the questions that is being asked particularly by people who are on the receiving end of that change is: What happens when people have spent twenty or twenty-five years of their lives in a particular mill and all of a sudden they are told that new machinery is being introduced and their services are no longer needed. The position of a person being displaced, sometimes, is to say, "Fine, I'll go down the road." But there are others who say, "I've invested twenty-five years of my life in this. I'm forty-eight years old. I don't want to change jobs now; this is all I know. Where am I going to go now?" Those are the sorts of questions that are being asked and they are not being answered very well in our society, certainly not as well as they are being answered in places like Scandinavia, where the ability of people to maintain livelihoods and work at things they seem to enjoy is better than here. That's a serious question and there are no easy answers for it, either. On the other hand, does that mean that we should stop innovation, stop engineering work along certain lines because it might threaten to displace people? Professor Luria, this is an area that you are interested in.

LURIA: We are talking about questions. The question is to find answers. One of our colleagues [at MIT], Les Thurow, thinks the only solution is in national industrial planning. Instead of having chaos and anarchy in our national industrial life, in which manufacturers get together somewhere in the twenty-ninth or seventy-fourth floor of some New York building and decide how they're going to do it, have our government elect the people to make a national policy in the same way as they created in the sixties the so-called Great Society, which at least provided security for all ages. Now we have to provide security for work and for opportunity. This can only be done, I think (and I think Thurow is much more qualified than I as an economist), through national planning. You may, after all, call it a step to socialism. Well, I think we have to stop being afraid of words and having fetishes like free enterprises in which a few people can do what they want and all of the others can be thrown out of job after, as you say, twenty-five or thirty years. What they need is to begin to think of national planning.

NOTES

1. Chicago Century of Progress International Exposition, *Official Guidebook of the Fair* (Chicago, 1933), 11. Pertinent discussions are found in Lowell Tozer, "A Century of Progress, 1833–1933: Technology's Triumph Over Man," *American Quarterly* 4 (1952):81; Howard P. Segal, *Technological Utopianism in American Culture* (Chicago: University of Chicago Press, 1985); and Robert W. Rydell, "The Fan Dance of Science: American World's Fairs in the Great Depression," *Isis* 76 (1985):531.

2. See Beard's introduction to J. B. Bury, *The Idea of Progress* (New York: The MacMillan Co., 1932), xx–xxii. Also see Beard, ed., *A Century of Progress* (New York: Harper & Brothers, 1933), 3–19.

3. Leo Marx, "Are Science and Society Going in the Same Direction?" *Science, Technology, and Human Values* 8 (Fall 1983):7.

4. For entry into the literature about millennial Protestantism, Calvinist theology, and the popular belief in national destiny, see Donald G. Mathews, "The Second Great Awakening as an Organizing Process, 1780–1830—An Hypothesis," *American Quarterly* 31 (1969):23–43; Frederick Merk, *Manifest Destiny and Mission in American History* (New York: Alfred A. Knopf, 1963); Perry Miller, *The Life of the Mind in America from the Revolution to the Civil War* (New York: Harcourt, Brace & World, 1965); Russel B. Nye, *Society and Culture in America, 1830–1860* (New York: Harper & Row, 1974), 1–31; Ernest C. Tuveson, *Redeemer Nation: The Idea of America's Millennial Role* (Chicago: University of Chicago Press, 1968).

5. Ibid. In addition to Marx's essay, background information for this paragraph is drawn from Arthur A. Ekirch, Jr., *The Idea of Progress in America, 1815–1860* (New York: Columbia University Press, 1944; New York: Peter Smith, 1951), 11–38; Russel B. Nye, "The American Idea of Progress," in *This Almost Chosen People: Essays in the History of American Ideas*, ed. R. B. Nye (East Lansing, Mich.: Michigan State University Press, 1966), 1–40; Nannerl O. Keohane, "The Enlightenment Idea of Progress Revisited," in *Progress and Its Discontents*, ed. G. A. Almond, M. Chodorow, and R. H. Pearce (Berkeley: University of California Press, 1982), 21–40; and Robert Nisbet, *History of the Idea of Progress* (New York: Basic Books, 1980), 3–167.

6. Thomas Jefferson, *Notes on the State of Virginia* (1785), as reprinted in *The Portable Thomas Jefferson*, ed. Merrill D. Peterson (New York: The Viking Press, 1975), 217.

7. Robert S. Woodbury, "The Legend of Eli Whitney and Interchangeable

Parts," *Technology and Culture* 1 (Summer 1960):243–44; Thomas Jefferson to John Melish, January 13, 1813, and to Benjamin Austin, January 9, 1816, reprinted in *The Philosophy of Manufactures: Early Debates Over Industrialization in the United States*, ed. Michael B. Folsom and Steven D. Lubar (Cambridge, Mass.: The MIT Press, 1982), 30–32.

8. Informative treatments of Jefferson's political economy are found in Leo Marx, *The Machine in the Garden* (New York: Oxford University Press, 1964); and Drew R. McCoy, *The Elusive Republic* (Chapel Hill, N.C.: University of North Carolina Press, 1980).

9. On the Waltham-Lowell system, see Caroline F. Ware, *The Early New England Cotton Manufacture* (Boston: Houghton Mifflin Co., 1931) and Thomas Dublin, *Women at Work* (New York: Columbia University Pres, 1979). On Hall, see Merritt Roe Smith, *Harpers Ferry Armory and the New Technology* (Ithaca, N.Y.: Cornell University Press, 1977). On the Erie Canal and the Transportation Revolution, see George R. Taylor, *The Transportation Revolution 1815– 1860* (New York: Holt, Rinehart and Winston, 1951).

10. Worth noting here is that the rhetoric of a society's falling away from old, traditional values was a familiar and often-repeated device by the early nineteenth century. Most prerevolutionary jeremiads repeated some variations of this lament. In fact, most Anglo-American settlers seem to have started casting off old norms and beliefs almost as soon as they stepped ashore. A number of scholars have pointed out that such rhetoric often obscures complex social experiences related to the rise of mercantile, and then industrial, capitalism. To be sure, the profit motive was always there, and so too were various ideologies and systems of belief to justify (and perhaps elevate) that motive. Each of America's major periods of adjustment to capitalist development (first through trade, then through industrial manufacturing, and perhaps now through computer automation) thus appears to have been accompanied by a crisis in ideology. Each crisis, in turn, inspired laments of falling away from "spiritual anchors," followed by the appearance of new or altered frames of belief. See, for example, Paul S. Boyer and Stephen Nissenbaum, *Salem Possessed: The Social Origins of Witchcraft* (Cambridge, Mass.: Harvard University Press, 1974); Gary B. Nash, *The Urban Crucible* (Cambridge, Mass.: Harvard University Press, 1979); Bernard Bailyn, *The Ideological Origins of the American Revolution* (Cambridge, Mass.: Harvard University Press, 1967); Sacvan Bercovitch, *The American Jeremiad* (Madison, Wis.: University of Wisconsin Press, 1978); and David F. Noble, *America by Design: Science, Technology, and the Rise of Corporate Capitalism* (New York: Alfred A. Knopf, 1977). I am indebted to Michael Smith for bringing this point to my attention.

11. Tench Coxe, *An Address to an Assembly of the Friends of American Manufactures, Convened for the Purpose of Establishing a Society for the Encouragement of Manufactures and the Useful Arts, Read in the University of Pennsylvania, on Thursday the 9th of August 1787* (Philadelphia, 1787), reprinted in Folsom and Lubar, *The Philosophy of Manufactures*, 61–62. For a perceptive treatment of technology in the early republic, see John F. Kasson, *Civilizing the Machine* (New York: Viking Press, 1976), 3–51.

12. Coxe, *Address*, 55. For further documentation, see Coxe, "An Enquiry into the Principles on Which a Commercial System for the United States of America Should Be Founded," *American Museum* 1 (1787):432–35; Coxe, *A View of the United States of America* (Philadelphia: William Hall, and Wrigley & Berriman, 1794); Jacob E. Cooke, *Tench Coxe and the Early Republic* (Chapel

Hill, N.C.: University of North Carolina Press, 1978), esp. 98–108, 182–216, 488–508; and Marx, *The Machine in the Garden*, 150–69, 180–82.

13. Coxe, *Address*, 55.

14. See, for example, Douglas T. Miller, *The Birth of Modern America, 1820–1850* (New York: Pegasus, 1970); Smith, *Harpers Ferry Armory;* Dublin, *Women at Work;* Philip Scranton, *Proprietary Capitalism: The Textile Manufacture at Philadelphia, 1800–1885* (New York: Cambridge University Press, 1983); and Jonathan Prude, *The Coming of Industrial Order* (New York: Cambridge University Press, 1983).

15. "Works and Days," in *Emerson's Works*, vol. 7, *Society and Solitude* (Boston: Houghton, Mifflin and Co., 1870), 158; Miller, *The Birth of Modern America*, 32; Greeley, ed., *Art and Industry at the Crystal Palace* (New York: Redfield, 1853), 52–53. Also see Hugo A. Meier, "Technology and Democracy, 1800–1860," *Mississippi Valley Historical Review* 43 (1957):618–40; Russel B. Nye, *Society and Culture in America, 1830–1860*, 3–31, 258; Nye, *This Almost Chosen People*, 1–42; and Ekirch, *The Idea of Progress in America*, 52, 106–31.

16. *Emerson's Works*, vol. 7, *Society and Solitude*, 166. On Emerson's changing views about technological change and industrialization, see Marx, *The Machine in the Garden*, 230–242. Also see Nye, *Society and Culture in America*, 275–77. Also relevant is Edward Bellamy, "Overworked Children in Our Mills," Springfield *Daily Union*, 5 June 1873, 2.

17. See Smith, *Harpers Ferry Armory;* Anthony F. C. Wallace, *Rockdale* (New York: Alfred A. Knopf, 1978); Michael H. Frisch and Daniel J. Walkowitz, eds., *Working-Class America: Essays on Labor, Community, and American Society* (Urbana, Ill.; University of Illinois Press, 1983), esp. 1–77; and Bruce Laurie, *Working People of Philadelphia, 1800–1850* (Philadelphia: Temple University Press, 1980).

18. Documentation on this point is abundant. See, for example, *Eighty Years' Progress of the United States, From the Revolutionary War to the Great Rebellion* (New York: L. Stebbins, New National Publishing House, 1864); Benson J. Lossing, *The American Centenary: A History of the Progress of the Republic of the United States During the First One Hundred Years of Its Existence* (Philadelphia: Porter and Coates, 1876); James P. Boyd, *Triumphs and Wonders of the 19th Century* (Chicago: C. W. Stanton Co., 1899); and Edward W. Byrn, *Progress of Inventions in the Nineteenth Century* (New York: Munn & Co., 1900).

19. *The Education of Henry Adams* (1918; reprint. Boston: Houghton Mifflin Company, 1974), 380; Adams to Charles Francis Adams, 11 April 1862, reprinted in *The Letters of Henry Adams*, ed. J. C. Levenson et al., 3 vols. (Cambridge, Mass.: Harvard University Press, 1982), 1:290.

20. In addition to the works cited in note 14, see also Herbert Gutman, *Work, Culture, and Society in Industrializing America* (New York: Vintage Books, 1977); Hugh G. J. Aitken, *Scientific Management in Action* (Cambridge, Mass.: 1985); Noble, *America by Design;* Merritt Roe Smith, ed., *Military Enterprise and Technological Change* (Cambridge, Mass.: The MIT Press, 1985); Martin J. Sherwin, *A World Destroyed: The Atomic Bomb and the Grand Alliance* (New York: Random House, 1975); Paul Boyer, *By the Bomb's Early Light: American Thought and Culture at the Dawn of the Atomic Age* (New York: Pantheon Books, 1985); Lewis Mumford, *Technics and Civilization* (1934; reprint, New York: Harcourt, Brace & World, 1963); and Ruth S. Cowan, *More Work for Mother* (New York: Basic Books, 1983).

21. For appraisals of the place of the auto in American culture, see James J.

Flink, "Three Stages of American Automobile Consciousness," *American Quarterly* 24 (1972): 451–73; Flink, *The Car Culture* (Cambridge, Mass.: The MIT Press, 1975); Robert S. Lynd and Helen M. Lynd, *Middletown* (New York: Harcourt, Brace & Co., 1929), 251–71; Blaine Brownell, "A Symbol of Modernity: Attitudes Toward the Automobile in Southern Cities in the 1920s," *American Quarterly* 24 (1972):20–44; and Reynold M. Wik, *Henry Ford and Grass Roots America* (Ann Arbor, Mich.: University of Michigan Press, 1972).

22. Quoted by Flink, "Three Stages," 456. Also see Henry Ford and Samuel Crowther, *My Life and Work* (Garden City, N.Y.: Doubleday, Page & Co., 1922).

23. Daniel J. Boorstin, *The Americans: The Democratic Experience* (New York: Random House, 1973), 548; Beard, *A Century of Progress*, 66; Ford, *My Life and Work*, introduction, esp. 10.

24. For descriptions of Ford's mass production system, see Stephen Meyer III, *The Five Dollar Day: Labor Management and Social Control in the Ford Motor Company, 1908–1921* (Albany: State University of New York Press, 1981), 9–65; and David A. Hounshell, *From the American System to Mass Production* (Baltimore: Johns Hopkins University Press, 1984), 217–301.

25. Hounshell, *From the American System*, 319–20.

26. Meyer, *The Five Dollar Day*, 79–83.

27. Ibid., 115, 119–31.

28. Ibid., 162, 170–71.

29. Ibid., 200–01.

30. Smith, *Military Enterprise*, 4–37, 331, 340–45; and David F. Noble, *Forces of Production: A Social History of Industrial Automation* (New York: Alfred A. Knopf, 1984). On the "Second Industrial Revolution," a phrase that refers to the rise of science-based industries and industrial research during the late nineteenth century, see Noble, *America by Design;* Thomas P. Hughes, *Networks of Power: Electrification in Western Society, 1880–1930* (Baltimore: Johns Hopkins University Press, 1983); and Leonard S. Reich, *The Making of American Industrial Research* (New York: Cambridge University Press, 1985).

31. Harley Shaiken, *Work Transformed: Automation and Labor in the Computer Age* (New York: Holt, Rinehart and Winston, 1985), 4–5, 47–48, 82, 146, 153, 247, 262–63. For an enlightening analysis of mass production and its socioeconomic implications, as well as the presentation of an alternative model of industrial development based on "flexible specialization," see Michael J. Piore and Charles F. Sabel, *The Second Industrial Divide* (New York: Basic Books, 1984).

32. Shaiken, *Work Transformed*, 128–35, 151–53, 178, 182.

33. Ibid., 243, 260–61.

34. Ibid., xiv, 277–78; Lewis Mumford, "Authoritarian and Democratic Technics," *Technology and Culture* 5 (1964):1–8; Langdon Winner, "Do Artifacts Have Politics?" *Daedalus* 109 (Winter 1980):121–36.

35. Carl Becker, "What Is Still Living in the Political Philosophy of Thomas Jefferson?" *American Historical Review* 48 (1943):691–706, esp. 702.

36. Keohane, "Progress Revisited," 40; Sheldon Wolin, "From Progress to Modernization: The Conservative Turn," *Democracy* 3 (Fall 1983):9–21.

37. Smith, *Military Enterprise*, 36–37, 345–46.

2. Genetic Progress and Religious Authority: Historical Reflections

DANIEL J. KEVLES

In June 1983, fifty-nine clerics advanced a resolution urging that "efforts to engineer specific genetic traits into the germ line of the human species should not be attempted," or, in other words, that no genetic engineering of inheritable human traits should be done.[1] The resolution gained widespread attention, not least because its signers were remarkably ecumenical, including several rabbis, a number of Roman Catholic bishops, and the leaders of eleven Protestant denominations. Religiously, they ranged from fundamentalists to liberals, from Jerry Falwell, the head of the Moral Majority, to Bishop A. James Armstrong, then president of the National Council of Churches. Among them, too, was our fellow participant in this Nobel Conference, J. Robert Nelson, then professor of theology at Boston University.

At a press conference held at the Warwick Hotel in New York City on the day the resolution was released, Dr. Nelson and several other clerics insisted that the document was by no means to be taken as an attack against genetic science as such. Bishop Finis A. Crutchfield, president of the Council of Bishops of the United Methodist Church, also pointed out that his fellow clerics were not talking against "repairing physical defects in individuals," for example, by replacing the defective genes in bone marrow that produce sickle-cell anemia. What they opposed, Bishop Crutchfield stressed, was "the creation and manufacture of new forms of life"—that is, the alteration of the human species by genetic manipulation of the sperm or egg.[2] Avery

Post, president of the United Church of Christ, explained that remaking the human germ line would be "the ultimate presumption," an act of hubris. This is a time, he added, when our "ethics of responsibility" require us to exercise "the freedom *not* to use our technical powers."[3]

The clerics' demand was warmly received in many quarters. Seven distinguished scientists, including two Nobel laureates, joined in support of the resolution, and Senator Mark Hatfield had it printed in the *Congressional Record*. However, Congressman Albert Gore, Jr., of Tennessee, who had conducted many hearings on genetic engineering, called the clerical resolution "a hasty judgment" while another group of scientists and theologians were moved to declare it "unnecessary and misleading."[4] Indeed, among a number of scientifically knowledgeable observers, the resolution stirred a good deal of head scratching. For one thing, it was not clear why the clerical signers would object in principle to the elimination from a family's germ line of the gene for, say, Huntington's disease, so that no one in future generations would be threatened by it. For another, and far more important, the burden of the resolution addressed a genetic fantasy.

The fact of the matter is that no one knows just what genes are responsible for the vast majority of human traits, particularly those that involve qualities of mind and behavior, and the techniques for genetically engineering the human sex cells remain to be developed. Barring some miraculous and unexpected scientific advance, genetically engineering new and reproducible human life forms thus seems, at the minimum, decades away. Professor Alexander M. Capron of the University of Southern California Law School, an authority in the field of bioethics, understandably criticized the clerical resolution as alarmist because it treated "as matters of immediate concern things that are not immediate." Capron added, "It's like yelling fire when there is no fire. What there is is a smoldering ashtray with the fire department watching it."[5]

The resolution thus posed a puzzle: Why were these religious authorities from across the sectarian and theological spectrum moved to raise such an alarm—to cry fire when no fire exists? A number of them were, most likely, just grossly misinformed about what might soon be technically possible in human genetics. But some, like Dr. Nelson, were not misinformed; on the contrary, they were knowledgeable about the state of human and medical genetics. In their view, too little attention was being given to the issue of human genetic engineering, particularly amid the rapid pace of advance in the field. A presidential commission had been created in 1980 to deliberate upon such matters, but, having completed its work, had gone out of business a few months earlier. The knowledgeable clerics were eager to sustain discussion of the issue.

The fact remains that the resolution did not call for debate on human genetic engineering. It declared unequivocally that attempts to engineer genetic traits into the human germ line should not be attempted. A few of the signers later told the press that they did not know whether the ban should be permanent. Many others said that they opposed human germ-line engineering uncompromisingly, even to prevent the transmission of genetic diseases.

The issue of human germ-line engineering, I would like to suggest, struck a deep and sensitive nerve among the clerical signers. The concern of the clerics, Dr. Nelson wrote in an unpublished letter to the *New York Times*, derived from "religious convictions and theological concepts about the value and inviolability of each human life as God's creation."[6] Dr. Nelson has elsewhere observed that, despite all the success of science in stealing the Promethean fire, for centuries the Christian apologist could always aver that only God could create life or know its originating mystery. But since 1953, when the structure of DNA was published, that ultimate redoubt of theologians has become increasingly vulnerable. To cite the shrewd observation of a report by the National Council of Churches, "Words which once were the primary language of the church are now also the words of the current biological revolution. Life, Death, Creation, New life, New day, New earth are now the vocabularies of biological science, biotechnology, and biobusiness."[7] What lay behind the imbroglio of the clerical resolution, I should like to propose, was an understandable desire on the part of its clerical signers to reassert, against scientific and secular challenge, the dominion of God over the mystery of life and the control of its creation. It arose from an increasing conflict between clerical and scientific authority over the ageless question: What are human beings, and what may human beings become?

THE GOSPEL OF EUGENICS

The conflict is, of course, one of long standing, and in the modern era it goes back to Charles Darwin's challenge to the comfortable belief that human beings were special creatures of God's creation and his insistence that they were, instead, simply other creatures of nature, cousins of the apes and subject to the same biological laws as their hairy relations. But while Darwin dealt heretically with the question of what men and women are, he did not take up the issue of what they might become. That question, which is more central to my inquiry here, was first raised, in 1865, by the English scientist Francis Galton.

Galton was a younger first cousin of Charles Darwin's, and he was inspired to raise the question in part by his reading of *On the Origin of Species.* It was well known that by careful selection farmers and flower fanciers could obtain valuable breeds of plants and animals strong in particular characters. Galton wondered, "Could not the race of men be similarly improved? Could not the undesirables be got rid of and the desirables multiplied?"[8] Could not human beings actually take charge of their own evolution? Galton developed his ideas for human improvement into a doctrine for which, in 1883, he coined the word *eugenics,* the word from a Greek root meaning "good in birth" or "noble in heredity." By eugenics, Galton intended to denote the "science" of improving human stock by giving "the more suitable races or strains of blood a better chance of prevailing speedily over the less suitable."

As did many mid-Victorians, Francis Galton made a religion of science. His religious attitudes ranged from skepticism to hostility. He once tested the efficacy of prayer by investigating whether or not groups for whom people prayed a good deal— for example, members of the royal family—outlived others, and he embarrassed his family by publishing the conclusion that since they did not, prayer must be inefficacious. In eugenics—

in the science of human improvement—Galton found a scientific substitute for church orthodoxies, a secular faith, a defensible religious obligation.

In the late nineteenth century, Galton's eugenics ideas provoked the opposition of clerics and won few lay supporters. Part of the reason was that science did not know of a hereditary mechanism that might be manipulated to the end of human improvement. Galton's gospel of eugenics received a considerable boost, however, when at the turn of this century the work of Gregor Mendel was rediscovered. One of the chief features of Mendel's laws, as they were understood early in the century, was that various biological characters were determined by single elements—which were later identified with genes. After the turn of the century, some scientists extrapolated this model of heredity to human beings, making two important points: First, they said that not only could such physical characteristics as eye color or disease be explained in terms of Mendel's elements, but that so also could characteristics of mind and behavior—for example, mental deficiency or even tendencies to criminality—which at the time were indiscriminately lumped under the vague term "feeblemindedness." Second, they argued that humankind might interfere with the propagation of these elements to increase the frequency of good ones in the population and decrease that of bad ones.

During the three decades or so after 1900, the secular faith of eugenics became a powerful and popular socioscientific gospel in the United States and Britain. Year after year, numerous books and articles were published on eugenics, and many public lectures were given on the subject. Many eugenics organizations were formed, among them, in 1923, the American Eugenics Society. The society's multifarious activities included holding Fitter Families contests, started in 1920 at the Kansas Free Fair. The contests were soon being featured—together with eugenics exhibits—at between seven and ten state fairs yearly; by the end of the decade, requests for help in organizing such contests were coming to the society each year from more than forty eager sponsors.

At the state fairs, the Fitter Families competitions were held in the "human stock" sections. "The time has come," a contest

Exhibit of the American Eugenics Society at the Kansas Free Fair, 1929. *(All photographs in this chapter are from the American Philosophical Society Library, Philadelphia. Used with permission.)*

The H. J. Lilly Family, winners in the "large family" class in the Fitter Families contest at the Arkansas State Fair, 1927.

brochure explained, "when the science of human husbandry must be developed, based on the principles now followed by scientific agriculture, if the better elements of our civilization are to dominate or even survive." At the 1924 Kansas Free Fair, winning families in the three categories—small, average, and large—were awarded the Governor's Fitter Family Trophy, presented by Governor Jonathan Davis. "Grade A Individuals" won a Capper Medal, named for United States Senator Arthur Capper and portraying two diaphanously garbed parents, their arms outstretched toward their (presumably) eugenically meritorious infant. A fair brochure noted: "This trophy and medal are worth more than livestock sweepstakes or a Kansas oil well. For health is wealth and a sound mind in a sound body is the most priceless of human possessions."[9]

The newfound popularity of eugenics was rife with religiosity, some of it—though not all of it—secular. In 1926 the American Eugenics Society published a pamphlet that it chose to title "A Eugenics Catechism." In question-and-answer format, the catechism promised that eugenics would "increase the number of geniuses," foster "more selective love-making," and produce more love in marriage. And the catechism continued:

Q. Does eugenics contradict the Bible?
A. The Bible has much to say for eugenics. It tells us that men do not gather grapes from thorns and figs from thistles. . . .
Q. What is the most precious thing in the world?
A. The human germ plasm.[10]

Francis Galton had expected eugenics to provide a secular substitute for traditional religion, and in the opening decades of the twentieth century, it was said to have accomplished just that. One of the leading scientific popularizers of the day was Albert E. Wiggam, a journalist, chautauqua lecturer, and author of magazine articles and widely read books, including the 1923 best-seller *The New Decalogue of Science*. There Wiggam intoned that the instruments of divine revelation were now the instruments of science. These instruments, he said, had "not only added an enormous range of new commandments—an entirely new Decalogue—to man's moral codes, but they have supplied him with the techniques for putting the old ones into effect."

According to Wiggam, salient among the new commandments was eugenics, which he summarized as "simply the projection of the Golden Rule down the stream of protoplasm." Indeed, he went on, had Jesus returned in the 1920s, he would have given the world a new commandment amounting to "the biological Golden Rule, the completed Golden Rule of science." This was, Wiggam declared, *"Do unto both the born and the unborn as you would have both the born and the unborn do unto you."*[11]

Particularly striking about the popularity of the eugenic faith at this time was that, in contrast to Galton's day, it had the enthusiastic cooperation of many clerics, known as modernists, who adhered to a theology that interpreted the Bible in accord with modern scientific and historical knowledge. In Britain, William Inge, the dean of St. Paul's Cathedral, helped to carry the eugenic banner to the British public, telling an audience at the Bedford College for Women that some knowledge of eugenics would "in many cases prevent falling in love with the wrong people."[12] In 1926, the American Eugenics Society was moved to launch a eugenic-sermon contest. An estimated three hundred sermons were inspired by the competition, and some sixty were considered for the prizes—of five hundred, three hundred, and two hundred dollars. Rabbi Harry H. Mayer, of Kansas City, Missouri, chose a special Mother's Day service convoked by the Council of Jewish Women and the Temple Sisterhood to declare, "May we do nothing to permit our blood to be adulterated by infusions of blood of inferior grade." Another entrant held that Christ was born into a family representing "a long process of religious and moral selection."[13]

The Reverend Dr. Kenneth C. MacArthur of the Federated Church in Sterling, Massachusetts, sermonized upon the heritability of intelligence and speculated that moral and spiritual qualities were similarly determined, submitting in evidence the biblical words of Paul to Timothy which celebrated, in his paraphrase, "the unfeigned faith which dwelt first in thy grandmother Lois, and thy mother Eunice; and in thee also." The Reverend Dr. MacArthur, whose sermon won second prize, later became a member of the society's Massachusetts branch and informed the society's president that he had been deeply interested in eugenics for years, was concerned with problems of

Reverend Dr. Kenneth C. MacArthur and family—winners of the silver cup in the "average family" class in the Fitter Families contest at the Eastern States Exposition, 1924.

genetics as a breeder of purebred cattle, and was the proud winner of a silver cup in the Fitter Families contest at the Eastern States Exposition of 1924.[14]

Fully to explain the immense popularity of eugenics during the first third of this century would require a separate paper. A couple of reasons stand out, however, that bear upon the enthusiasm that so many clerics exhibited. First, science as such had come to command enormous authority, having conferred numerous technological marvels upon the world since the late nineteenth century. Many clerics felt compelled to align themselves with the modernist doctrine of harmonizing religion and morals with the methods of science and the known laws of nature. Second, the eugenics of the day gave little attention to what had preoccupied Galton—that is, to creating superior people, to humanity's taking charge of its own evolution. A major reason for this was that geneticists at the time knew far less than the little they do today about how one might achieve such an end. No one knew what genes consisted of or how they replicated themselves, let alone how they might be deliberately modified to engineer better human beings. Thus, eugenics for the most part did not directly challenge traditional clerical authority over the nature and possibilities of humanity.

To be sure, eugenicists did propose to interfere with human reproduction with the aim of preventing the proliferation of alleged genetic "defectives"—a policy that science seemed to sanction. Because of Mendel's laws, it was argued, the breeding of such people would surely cause the genetic pollution of "the race." Consider, for example, some of the charts displayed at the Kansas Free Fair in 1929 that purported to illustrate the "laws" of Mendelian inheritance in human beings: Cross a "pure" with a "pure" parent, and the children would be "normal," they said. But cross an "abnormal" with an "abnormal," and the children would be "abnormal." Cross a "pure" with an "abnormal," and the children would be "normal but tainted; some grandchildren abnormal." Cross a "tainted" with a "tainted," and of every four offspring one would be "abnormal," one "pure normal," and two "tainted." Typically, the exhibit included a depiction of the laws of Mendelian inheritance—usually a collection of stuffed black and white guinea pigs arrayed on a vertical board so as to indicate the inheritance of coat color from generation to generation. Another chart declared, "Unfit human traits such as feeblemindedness, epilepsy, criminality, insanity, alcoholism, pauperism, and many others run in families and are inherited in exactly the same way as color in guinea pigs." An exhibit placard asked, "How long are we Americans to be so careful for the pedigree of our pigs and chickens and cattle, and then leave the *ancestry of our children* to chance, or to 'blind' sentiment?"[15]

All these social pathologies were said to be increasing at a terrible rate. At the Sesquicentennial Exposition in Philadelphia, in 1926, the American Eugenics Society exhibit included a board that, in the manner of the population counters of a

The American Eugenics Society exhibits at the Sesquicentennial Exposition, held in Philadelphia in 1926. The guinea pig pelts on the board on the right were used to depict the laws of Mendelian inheritance.

This board, exhibited at Philadelphia's Sesquicentennial Exposition in 1926, used flashing lights to denote the proliferation of births of "deficient" human beings and the financial burden that they imposed on the "fit."

later day, revealed with flashing lights that every fifteen seconds one hundred dollars of the taxpayer's money went for the care of persons with bad heredity, that every forty-eight seconds a mentally deficient person was born in the United States, and that only every seven and a half minutes did the United States enjoy the birth of "a high-grade person . . . who will have ability to do creative work and be fit for leadership."[16]

In the United States, the "feebleminded," criminals, and other such social "defectives" were believed to occur with disproportionately high frequency among recent immigrants from eastern and southern Europe. Two major methods that American eugenicists advocated for ridding society of these sources of social pathology were immigration restriction and compulsory sterilization. Eugenicists in fact helped obtain passage of the Immigration Restriction Act of 1924, which sharply reduced eastern and southern European immigration to the United States. They also played a major role in the passage of eugenic sterilization laws in some two dozen states by the late 1920s, and they succeeded in having such legislation declared constitutional in the 1927 U.S. Supreme Court decision *Buck* v. *Bell*.

With regard to the position of religious leaders on these eugenic measures, some opposition to immigration restriction seems to have come from Jewish clerics, but no religious group matched the across-the-board attack against eugenics that came from the Roman Catholic Church. The Catholic dissent rested intellectually on the church's doctrine that in the scheme of God's creation the bodily attributes of men and women are secondary, their spirits paramount. What to the eugenicists were biologically unfit people were to the church the children of God, blessed with immortal souls and entitled to the respect due every human being. In 1931, Pope Pius XI, in the encyclical *Casti Connubii*, condemned eugenics and sterilization along with birth control and divorce. But the American Catholic dissent from eugenics was reinforced by social reasons. A disproportionately large number of prospective immigrants from eastern and southern Europe were Catholic. And so were a disproportionately large number of those threatened with compulsory eugenic sterilization—because Catholic immigrants tended to fall among lower-income groups, to be less educated than native

Americans, to score poorly on the I.Q. tests used to classify people as feebleminded or not, and to be sent to public—rather than private—institutions for the mentally deficient, to whose inmates, and whose inmates alone, eugenic sterilization laws could be applied.

Opposition to immigration restriction or eugenic sterilization may have come from fundamentalist Protestants, too, but little scholarly knowledge of that matter exists yet. No significant opposition seems to have come from modernist Protestant clerics, who virtually ceded their moral authority in this area to those who spoke in the name of eugenic science. For one thing, in the United States the principal supporters of eugenics in the first third of the twentieth century were middle- to upper-middle-class WASPs—white Anglo-Saxon Protestants—who liked to trace their lineage back to northern Europe and England. It should be no surprise that WASP ministers shared the views of their WASP congregants. Those views tended to include an anti-Catholicism so virulent at the time as to relegate large numbers of Catholics to virtually subhuman categories. And what social prejudice created, the science of genetics, some claimed, confirmed. Henry H. Goddard, a eugenicist, was the psychologist who pioneered the use of I.Q. tests in the United States to diagnose "feeblemindedness." In his influential books on the subject, Goddard speculated that feeblemindedness expressed a form of reversion to a more primitive level of humanity: "a vigorous animal organism of low intellect but strong physique— the wild man of today."[17] Thus, modernist Protestant clerics did not fear eugenics as a challenge to their authority over the nature of human beings and their future for the simple reason, I would suggest, that to their minds the objects of eugenic programs—Catholic immigrants, the "feebleminded," and so on—fell de facto outside the realms of humanity.

CLERICAL ACTIVISM AND THE NEW EUGENICS

By the mid-1930s, public opinion—both lay and clerical—in Britain and the United States was turning sharply against eugenics. Revulsion over the Nazi eugenic program had a good deal to do with the shift. So did developments in genetics and psychology, demonstrating that the attribution of "feeblemind-edness" or social deviancy so casually and completely to genetic causes was for the most part wrong. And so, finally, did the explosive growth from the 1930s onward of knowledge of human heredity as a special branch of genetics. But that knowledge, combined with the advance of medical technology, has in the last decade or so brought us to the edge of what some have called a new eugenics, to the borderlands of a brave new world of genetic and reproductive behavior, to the prospects that so bothered the fifty-nine clerics in June 1983.

Clerical opinion in the three major faiths is divided on various features of the new reproductive and genetic possibilities, particularly those that represent sharp departures from ancient practice. Most Jews and liberal Protestants approve amniocentesis and abortion to permit prospective parents to avoid the birth of children with serious diseases and disorders, but this innovation has been vigorously opposed by Catholics and fundamentalist Protestants. Artificial insemination by donor, surrogate motherhood, and in vitro fertilization may assist otherwise infertile couples to have children; all three techniques have earned the censure of the Catholic Church. Against this division of opinion, the broad clerical consensus against attempts genetically to engineer new human beings stands out all the more sharply.

The canvas of history throws the reason for this consensus into bold relief. Unlike the old eugenics, the new variety has so far—for the most part—relegated no particular minority group to the level of subhumanity while keeping the majority safe; it promises to be universal, to affect everyone. Thus, clerics of *all* faiths and social groups are naturally concerned to prevent the cruelties and barbarities of the old eugenics from recurring. Then, too, the precedent of nuclear energy strongly suggests the need for moral voices to raise a cautionary note against any headlong exploitation of new scientific knowledge, and so does the contemporary rapid rush to commercialize molecular biology and biotechnology. Finally, the more that genetic progress strikes at clerical authority over the nature of men and women, the more do clerics have a professional self-interest in not yielding to scientists' ultimate authority over humanity's essence and fate.

What should we think of this clerical activism—this revived religious concern with the issues of God, humanity, and genetics? In my opinion, we should welcome it. Let us recall that some geneticists invoked the authority of their science to establish the eugenics of the early twentieth century. Let us also note that a degree of hubris is to be found in some of the proclamations by scientists nowadays of new genetic imperatives. We may well applaud the Catholic dissent from eugenics of half a century ago. Similarly, we might gladly welcome contemporary clerical activism. Clerical opinion reflects deep-seated feelings that are found in most of us against tampering with the ultimate mystery of life. If neither the science nor the technology currently exists to transform ourselves, that does not render our feelings about such issues any less real.

Clerical involvement in human genetics and biotechnology, however, must go hand in hand with considerable technical knowledge—which, I am pleased to say, an increasing number of clerics are beginning to acquire. Genetic progress is not so much undermining religious authority as demanding a modification of its basis and content. That same genetic progress is also demanding of the geneticist an unprecedented degree of moral sensitivity. In all, authority over the nature of humanity and its possibilities now belongs neither to the scientist nor to the cleric alone. It belongs to both, and to all the rest of us—and it will be shared all the more as the rapid advances of our genetic knowledge and biotechnical capacity touch ever more deeply and concretely our sense of ourselves, what we are, and what we may become.

PANEL DISCUSSION

NELSON: David Baltimore, another Nobel laureate, also criticized the 1983 statement, asking why we were not compassionate. It is a very legitimate question because people who lead churches are supposed to be compassionate. Compassion is not lacking for those with genetic diseases, nor is there any desire to see the continuation of these diseases. What we were concerned about, then, was the inadvertent mutations that would be caused if the technique of germ-line modification could indeed be perfected, because those inadvertent mutations (according to the best authorities I read) would be irreversible and irrevocable throughout the continuing line of one's progeny.

Now that's a theoretical fantasy, in the words of Dr. Kevles, but we wondered about the outcomes of what appear to be scientific fantasies. Many of us have grown up in a time when scientific fantasies have become realities. Ten or twelve years ago, few people would have anticipated through fantasy or imagination what has been done in recombinant DNA technology and the spread of the knowledge of the genetic sciences. What I'm saying is that to dismiss an apprehension as a fantasy is not altogether convincing, simply because we have come to recognize the acceleration, rapidity, and astonishing achievement in this area.

Recently, I was on a commission of the Office of Technology Assessment in Washington. There a group of responsible geneticists and other scientists worked out a long report concerning the therapeutic treatment of genetic diseases in the somatic cells as distinct from the sex or germ cells. Even in that report the word *inadvertent* appears several times—the inadvertent mutation of genes that could then be passed on to the future. What we are dealing with, essentially, is the constant problem that is before scientific experimentation—that is, the problem of risk to human beings. That raises the whole question of whether there can be advances, especially in medical science and now in genetic science, without assuming risks to certain human subjects that later on might prove to have been very unsatisfactory.

KEVLES: I really do not understand the specter you raise of modifying the germ line in a way that will go on for generations. If you accept the premise that you can modify the germ line for a desirable change, and a change ensues you don't like, then you can modify it back. The technology that can do one will permit you to do the next.

A second point regards the clerical resolution, an entire issue that I chose to neglect in my paper. It seems to me by focusing on what I call (and I think most people agree is) a genetic fantasy, attention is diverted from the imminent genetic reality of somatic cell modification. The NIH recently issued regulations to govern the procedures to be followed in somatic cell modifications. An enormous number of ethical and moral problems as well as technical ones are going to arise with the advent of somatic cell therapy. I am puzzled, because to focus on what is decades away diverts attention from what is real and imminent and requires considerable attention from moralists, theologians, ethicists, scientists, and even historians.

NELSON: The advent of the kind of information that you have mentioned is something that cannot and will not be suppressed. It has to be used, however, in a way that is entirely to the benefit of the individual who may suffer from this [congenital disease] and his or her family, but especially the individual. The acquisition of new information concerning our faith, so to speak, of a biomedical and genetic nature is posing a widespread problem that goes far beyond genetics. In the biotechnological area there are problems in the prolongation of life at birth, and also the prolongation of life at death. What shall we do with these techniques and this information? I do not want to issue a blanket censure of the use of such information or of such techniques, but I would say that we have to figure out ways to use them in terms that will benefit rather than injure those who suffer from these problems. And that is where I think this kind of attention ought to be directed rather than to something that may happen fifty years or more from now.

LURIA: It seems to me that these kinds of controversy simply mean that there is a conflict between sets of values that are neither reconciled nor reconcilable. The two sets of values are, on the one hand, the desire to develop techniques that will satisfy even the slightest wish, such as correcting one's own heredity in favor of one's understanding. That is a legitimate desire. On the other hand, there is an equally legitimate desire, especially in light of what has happened in two world wars, to preserve the idea of something sacred about humanity as such, because without humanity this world will not have any meaning. Therefore, it seems to me there is a real conflict of values in our society between different kinds of goals and desires. That is what Dr. Kevles and Dr. Nelson are representing in this discussion.

BYRNE: Professor Kevles, would not genetic improvements only be possible for those who could afford the process, leaving the poor at a severe disadvantage?

KEVLES: This is again a special case of a more pervasive issue. I think that it would be wrongheaded to take the position that we should not have genetic progress, or progress in medicine or any other sort of technology because it may not be equitably distributed in the society. At the same time, care must also be taken, an effort must be made, to ensure it is equitably distributed in society. That is the only answer I can give.

NOTES

1. Resolution, June 8, 1983, copy in author's possession.
2. *New York Times,* June 9, 1983, 19.
3. J. Robert Nelson, "Genetic Science: A Menacing Marvel," *The Christian Century* (July 6–13, 1983): 636.
4. *Time,* June 20, 1983, 67; *New York Times,* August 7, 1983, 18.
5. *New York Times,* June 9, 1983, 19.
6. J. Robert Nelson to the *New York Times,* June 15, 1983, copy kindly supplied me by Dr. Nelson.
7. Julie Ann Miller, "The Clergy Ponder the New Genetics," *Science News* 125 (March 24, 1984), 190.
8. Karl Peason, *The Life, Letters, and Labours of Francis Galton* (Cambridge: Cambridge University Press, 1914–1930), 3:348.
9. *The Fitter Families Eugenic Competition at Fairs and Expositions* (American Eugenics Society, 1922); "Department S—Eugenics," from the Premium Book of the Kansas Free Fair, Topeka, September 8–13, 1924. Charles B. Davenport Papers, American Philosophical Society Library, Philadelphia, Pa., Cold Spring Harbor Series #2, Eugenics: Wiggam et al. file.
10. "A Eugenics Catechism" (American Eugenics Society, 1926), 2–3, 10.
11. Albert E. Wiggam, *The New Decalogue of Science* (New York: Bobbs-Merrill, 1923), 109–11.
12. *Morning Leader,* March 8, 1910, copy in Eugenics Society Press Clippings Scrapbook, Eugenics Society, London.
13. "Eugenics Sermon," 1926; Harry H. Mayer, "Eugenics, A Sermon for Mother's Day," May 9, 1926, American Eugenics Society Papers, American Philosophical Society Library, boxes 11, 14.
14. Kenneth C. MacArthur, "Eugenics Sermon," June 20, 1926; L. E. Whitney to MacArthur, July 20, 1927, American Eugenics Society Papers, box 14.
15. From photographs of the exhibits, American Eugenics Society Papers.
16. Ibid.
17. Henry H. Goddard, *Feeble-mindedness: Its Causes and Consequences* (New York: Macmillan, 1914), 504, 508–09.

3. The Single Artificer

SALVADOR E. LURIA

The reader may wonder whether the title of this essay refers to God, who was in fact called the Great Artificer by philosophers and Freemasons of the eighteenth century. They wished to keep God alive, but preferred to relegate His role to an initial creative impulse, after which God could relax and forever enjoy the show. Whether that happened with a big bang some twenty billion years ago or more quietly in 4000 B.C. is still a matter of dispute between physicists and creation scientists.

That is not my subject, however. What I wish to explore is a different kind of creation. The title I have chosen, "The Single Artificer," comes from one of the best-known poems by the American poet Wallace Stevens, "The Idea of Order at Key West." The poem begins with a line of great poetic power— "She sang beyond the genius of the sea"—followed by lovely lines that contrast human voice with the voice of the ocean.[1] *Meaning,* the poet tells us, comes into nature by and only by the activity of the human spirit. The noise of the sea becomes something more than just noise because *we* hear it and *we* interpret it. Likewise, I would add, plants and animals and the heavenly bodies acquire significance for us because human understanding imposes upon them an order—that is, a pattern of relations. The idea of a humanly imposed order is an old one. It appears early in the Book of Genesis, when Adam puts order into the chaos of living things by giving plants and animals names, surely a second act of creation.

Later in Stevens's poem my title appears: "She was *the single artificer* of the world / In which she sang."[2] The concept is now more precisely expressed: Creation is the result of human activity, of human performance. Order in the world emerges from active human involvement, from the unraveling of hidden relations between objects and events. Thus is the music revealed that is hidden underneath the noise of nature; and thus the story concealed in the strata of rocks and the layers of fossil bones becomes manifest.

This is the creation I wish to examine in this essay, the adventure of the human spirit: an adventure whose essence is communication, shared knowledge and shared emotion. This adventure is made possible by the unique qualities of human nature, by the evolution of human brain, human language, and human consciousness out of our animal past. It is this adventure that gives meaning and even purpose to individual human beings—a purpose here and now, not a purpose there and beyond; a purpose distinct from the pursuit of personal success as well as from the pursuit of personal salvation, because its meaning comes from participation in a collective enterprise, not from preparation for a personal afterlife.

MODES OF UNDERSTANDING

The central feature of this adventure is *understanding*—the search for meaning in the structures, events, and relationships that we encounter and perceive. Understanding is not a simple or unique operation, and the paths that lead to it can be diverse. We seek understanding through science, which provides explanations for the regularities of the material world. We seek understanding through art, which reveals to us forms and designs and abstractions that stir and focus our emotions because they resonate with hidden harmonies in our souls and make them sharable. And we seek understanding through history, philosophy, and literature, which explore our human past and our thinking processes. Within each of these realms—science, art, and humanities—are diverse modes of understanding, diverse devices, each with a long history and each with a distinct entitlement within the tradition of thought. I shall call these modes the rational, the unrational, and the irrational modes, which differ in their methods, their appeals, and their contributions. All paths to understanding—science, art, and the humanities—combine these three modes in various measures.

The rational mode searches for order, structure, and predictability. It does so by reasoning, as in philosophy and mathematics, and by experimentation, as in modern natural science. It attempts to weed out the irrational and to be on guard against mixing rational with unrational.

The unrational mode is the search for emotional experience, either creative or responsive. It is preeminently aesthetic and artistic. It does not seek order and reproducibility but rather intensity and uniqueness of experience. It seeks to respond to our quest for emotional fulfillment by revealing associations and feelings, and awakening resonances whose content cannot be rationalized or even put into words. This is true of music, of poetry, and of all those natural or artifactual phenomena that convey satisfying or provocative relations of form or color or pattern.

It is the unrational element of art that the philosopher Herbert Marcuse extolled when he suggested that "art must communicate a truth . . . not accessible to ordinary language and ordinary experience."[3] It all depends, of course, on what one chooses to call truth and objectivity. Marcuse wished to assign the value of truth to inner experiences that cannot be put into words and cannot therefore be communicated to others. But to conclude that such subjective experiences provide access to any higher objectivity at all, that the unrational is a higher form of rationality, hardly seems appropriate. The danger of this confusion is that it tends to legitimize all sorts of spurious, solipsistic beliefs provided they are coupled with strong emotional feelings. In the hands of psychiatrists such as R. D. Laing, the subjectivity of the psychotic becomes the only valid reality.[4]

This brings me to the irrational mode—the assertion of personal or sectarian pet theories as *explanations,* either for natural phenomena or for emotional reactions. At some times the irrational mode serves a useful purpose by stimulating the search for more effective solutions. For example, alchemy in the Middle Ages—the search for transmutation of elements—became the basis of modern chemistry. Science itself uses the irrational mode when scientists attempt in an almost perverse way to invent fantastic explanations as foils against which to test their constructs. Newton, for example, besides being the greatest scientist of his time, was also a religious crank, speculating about biblical hermeneutics. Can we exclude the possibility that his theological musing might have contributed in a dialectical manner to his greatest scientific insights?

Astrology was certainly a source of understanding in the days before modern science. By exploring the ancient beliefs in the connection between planetary motions and the course of human affairs, astrology helped the search for regular patterns in both domains, many centuries after rational philosophers such as Lucretius had already dismissed this kind of speculation as softheaded. But present-day astrology, alas, does not even claim to provide shortcuts to understanding. As we can read in almost any daily paper in the United States, astrology is now a commercial pursuit catering to ignorance and self-delusion and to the confusion of reality with wishful thinking. What could possibly be the link between the position of planets at the time of one's birth and the events one encounters on a certain day of the week or of the month? Yet, each week millions of Americans purchase astrological magazines, and millions presumably consult their daily horoscopes before making their decisions, perhaps even decisions that affect their own futures—or worse, if they happen to be in positions of power, decisions that may affect the future of a nation and of the world.

On a par with astrology, and possibly even less respectable because they tend to discredit serious science, are pseudo-sciences such as the study of extrasensory perception and telepathy, which surprisingly enough still prosper even in certain academic surroundings. Even professionally trained scientists have managed to persuade themselves that their subjects can predict and even "will" which card shall appear next to another in a properly shuffled deck, or make objects bend at a distance, or transmit thoughts by means that do not obey the inverse square law, by means of some kind of lasers of the mind. I always wonder why, if people possess such gifts, they do not make a killing on the stock market.

RELIGION AND UNDERSTANDING

These examples of irrational thinking are clearly outside the process of understanding. More interesting and instructive is the field of religion, which involves a remarkable admixture of rational, unrational, and irrational elements. Historically the function of religion has been to provide comfort to human beings who seek for meaning in their lives and struggle against a sense of futility and a terror of death: what existentialist philosophers call the absurd feature of human destiny, the tension between human consciousness and the awareness of personal transcience. The unrational, aesthetic contribution of religion is to fight despair by inventing for life a presumption of metaphysical significance, either the gift of elusion stemming from special creation or the promise of salvation in the form of an ultimate purpose, such as reward after death and immortality of the soul. Religion offers an excuse for life and a purpose for human existence. Even in its more ascetic form, religion provides emotional comfort by immersing the individual in communal rites and offering the support of shared experiences.

Yet, in attempting to invent meaning and purpose for human life within the universe, most religions have in the course of history invented explanations for the universe itself as experienced by human beings. They have created a mixture of the irrational, the unrational, and the rational: a mixture of threatening rules, comforting visions, and commonsense directives for everyday life. Within Christianity, the exercise *credo quia absurdum est*—"I believe it because it is absurd"—was applied not only to the idea of God and His work, but also to a cosmology and a natural history taken for granted because backed by authority. Thus religion, while striving to be the expounder of powers beyond human understanding, also became the tool of the controlling powers within society.

Not surprisingly, when modern science arose, the pseudoscience of religion refused to give ground; its scientific pretenses had become part of the power structure, an entitlement that gave its custodians social and political power. The earth had to continue to be the center of the universe if pope and emperor and kings and landlords were to continue in power in the name of God. Even in our present-day American culture, religion's pretenses go beyond the retelling of biblical stories as artistic creations. Organized religion insists on its cosmology and eschatology—whether the fanatic assertions of fundamentalist Christians or the fatalistic creed of the millenarians—being taken as revealed scientific truth. Not long ago a United States Secretary of the Interior who is a religious millenarian told a congressional committee that there may be no need to make plans beyond a few generations: the coming of the millennium will presumably wipe out or transform the existing world.[5] It is reassuring to realize that similar predictions failed in the year 1000; but some people clearly don't learn.

More threatening to the process of understanding are para-religious movements such as creation science, the belief that the words of Genesis are to be literally interpreted in the place of geology and biology and physics. Already, the legislatures in Arkansas and Louisiana have enthusiastically adopted creation science as an alternative to the Darwinian theory of evolution to be taught in public schools.[6] These legislators apparently failed to see the incompatibility between the timetable of Genesis and the age of the petroleum deposits whose exploitation they had presumably been elected to protect. Fortunately, thus far, federal courts have made short shrift of such aberrations in the two cases in question, ruling the legislation unconstitutional.[7] But, with all due respect to the judiciary, I am not convinced of the wisdom of depending on it to set things right once creation scientists have begun to rank evolutionary theory as one of their political targets along with abortion and homosexuality.

Before the rise of modern science the deliberate pursuit of rationality in the intellectual sphere was the prerogative of geometry and philosophy and history. The ancient philosophers readily allowed irrational beliefs to enter their work when dealing with natural phenomena that they could not explain. They were more concerned with the human mind and the human condition than with lightning and earthquakes. And they profited from the unrational—the aesthetic response elicited by the artistry of Plato and Lucretius or the robust texture of Aristotelian discourse. What the humanities did was to provide an alternate, more rational comfort than that of religion, a more objective sense of human life—a promise that understanding of the human condition, if not of human purpose, was at least potentially approachable by observing human thoughts and action. Dispelling the terror of natural forces as symbolized in the ancient gods, philosophers and historians provided understanding if not hope.

SHARED EXPERIENCE: THE SOURCE OF MEANING

With the rise of Christianity in the Western world, the dichotomy between salvation and damnation as embodied in St. Augustine's doctrine became central to the societal view of the human predicament. But when the promise of salvation came to be seen as hollow, when the traditional institutions warranted by theology started to crumble, personal despair became a widespread emotion of humankind in modern times. Existential despair flourished on the ashes of eighteenth-century optimism when the era of revolution ended not in a world of community but in a world of individualism and its ultimate product, metaphysical nationalism.

One of the most terrifying visions of human despair and futility that literature can convey is contained in Samuel Beckett's story *The Lost Ones,* presumably an allegory of the human condition.[8] A throng of individuals is imprisoned in an immense cavern. They have no implements but a set of tall ladders. One by one, without any organized plan, the lost ones climb whatever ladder becomes available, even struggling for possession of a ladder, and seek to find escape by digging in tunnels none of which has ever led to a breakthrough. The lost ones never cooperate. The exploration done by one of them never has any meaning for the others. All efforts yield nothing and mean nothing. The picture of life that Beckett conveys is one of solipsistic futility. Such a perseverance despite futility is even less meaningful and less inspiring than that of Sisyphus, for whom action, however futile, was a perennial challenge to fate. In *The Lost Ones,* Beckett raises the question of personal meaning and personal salvation and, finding none, sinks into utter despair.

What Beckett fails to convey, or rather conveys by contrast, is that meaning and salvation are not personal categories; they come only from participation in shared activity, in the collective enterprise of humanity. They come from commitments to shared values, communality, morality, and justice. The optimism of ancient and eighteenth-century philosophers came from the vision of societies dedicated to communal values.

Sartre's existential aphorism *l'enfer c'est les autres*—"hell is other people"—completely misses the point. On the contrary, life *is* the others, in the past and in the present. The sense of personal meaning comes from our shared response to the Parthenon, to Sophocles' tragedies, to Whitman's and Shakespeare's verses, and also from our sharing with others, past and present, the understanding of geometry and natural science and the enjoyment of art and of companionship. The artists and the scholars of the past whose work has meaning for us saw human life as an adventure: not the Augustinian adventure of preparation for an afterlife, but the adventure of understanding, expressing, and delighting in the world in which we live. Meaning and salvation come to us because we are adventurers: not lonely adventurers in search of a personal Shangri-la, but adventurers searching for shared experience, shared within family, within community, within humanity as a whole. Such a shared life makes the awareness of biological death tolerable as just another incident in the adventure of living. And the lasting part of the shared experience is the contribution that each of us makes to the collective adventure.

THE NATURE OF SCIENTIFIC UNDERSTANDING

Here I wish to limit my comments to the contributions of a certain subset of adventurers; those people think of as scientists, who try to discover and clarify reproducible patterns in the events and activities that they choose to explore. Modern science, starting in the sixteenth century when Galileo, Descartes, and Newton introduced the experimental method of exploration and verification, set itself a novel task, profoundly different from the geometry and the philosophy of the ancients. The goal was understanding of a new kind: to explain phenomena and events in terms of experimentally testable hypotheses rather than of ideal concepts. The first triumph was the explanation of planetary motion by Newton using Galileo's experimental method coupled with Descartes' analytical geometry. In place of the ideal circles and geometrical speculations down to Kepler's time in the seventeenth century, Newtonian mechanics introduced measurement and reduction to simple, generalizable statements dealing with forces, objects, and their motion.

Science, as it has grown since then, is founded on two main tenets. The first is the assumption that the processes of the human mind are in principle congruent with the structure of the natural world, including the structure and function of the human brain itself. This includes within modern science the scientific study of society and of the human mind but excludes from science—although of course not from philosophy—any distinction between physical and metaphysical reality. The second tenet of modern science is that no explanation should be taken as even tentatively correct unless it has been submitted to adequate tests—that is, tests whose results could actually or potentially disprove the explanation once and for all. An expressive way to put this is to say that modern science—in fact, science altogether—is perennially on guard against *wishful thinking*. Wishful thinking has to be examined and dispelled not only in its crudest forms, such as the belief in the efficacy of prayer in causing rain or the belief that a horseshoe on the wall can bring good luck, but also in its more subtle ways, where it takes the form of unexamined, intuitive commonsense assumptions. Einstein's crucial contribution to physics, for example, was to catch within the edifice of Newtonian physics the hidden commonsense belief that the time frame of events could be the same for any two observers irrespective of their relative motion—a seemingly reasonable assumption, yet, as it turned out, an unjustified one.

More generally, the path of modern science has consisted in going beyond the intuitive levels of explanation. Science proceeds by challenging intuition and advances by further and more subtle reexaminations of assumptions. It does not perversely question the edifice it has built, but when difficulties arise it reviews its hypotheses in search of hidden flaws. This is what happened when the science of electromagnetic waves caused Einstein to explore critically the hidden assumptions of Newtonian theory. And in both Newtonian and Einsteinian advances, the effectiveness of the new solutions was coupled with a kind of aesthetic beauty, a layer of unrational pleasure in pattern and order, and confidence in the ability of the human mind to expand beyond the limitations of our sense-limited intuitions.

Hidden assumptions, and especially personal and social biases, are easier to eliminate (or at least to ignore) in the natural sciences than in the social sciences, within which I would include everything from sociology to economics and most of medicine. These branches of science deal with human affairs much more directly than do physics or chemistry or biology. Motivations and findings are closer to human and social concern. The temptation to generalize and to apply incomplete knowledge reflects both the difficulty of duplicating sets of data and the urgency of the problem under study. Personal and social biases in choice of problems and interpretation of data are easily hidden or overlooked in dealing even at the research level with problems of intense relevance to society.

In the natural sciences, the direction of research is somewhat less influenced by the social context, even though the course of scientific discovery is inevitably influenced by social forces— demand for new technologies as well as economic factors that affect funds for research. Yet, once a science develops into a consistent, solid body of knowledge, its structure and direction are affected mainly by the internal dynamics of the subject matter itself rather than by the immediate demands of society. Scientists explore problems that arise in the course of their work and seem soluble at a given time with the means at hand, whether the means happen to be Cartesian geometry for Newton, or fruit flies or bacteria for twentieth-century geneticists, or synchrotrons or linear accelerators. In the words of one distinguished scientist, Sir Peter Medawar, science is the "art of the soluble."[9]

This apparently opportunistic course of natural science protects it to a certain extent from the biases and the turmoils of social pressure. But such a comforting sense of shelter, the illusion of pursuing a pure intellectual activity, not driven by practical goals, cannot hide the fact that all findings of science, all advances in scientific knowledge, are potentially sources of power over natural phenomena and can have (and do have) tremendous impact on human affairs and not only on human understanding. The content of science may, to a certain extent at least, be value free. But science itself is the product of a human society permeated with values—in fact, contradictory sets of values.

THE RELATIONSHIP OF SCIENCE TO TECHNOLOGY

In the earliest days of the Scientific Revolution, one of its greatest proponents, Francis Bacon, wrote the fateful words "knowledge is power." He thought of the newly emerging science in terms of power—abstract power over the forces of nature as well as political power in the society he was bent on ruling. The ambiguity of his statement must not have been as evident in the early seventeenth century as it is in the nuclear age.

The tie between understanding and power, between science-and-technology (a hyphenation often used by college presidents in search of subsidies), tends to obscure the profound difference between science—the understanding of natural phenomena—and technology. Science is in principle indifferent to technological applications. The landing of an astronaut on the moon or of a space vehicle on Mars had, for example, little to do with science. These exploits even used a minimum of science: They required only Newton's laws, transistor physics, and thermodynamics. The rest was technology—superbly sophisticated technology, to be sure, but not science.

I remember how scandalized Jerry Piel, the publisher of *Scientific American*, was when in a letter to the *New York Times* I stated that there was more scientific value in a newly published report on blue-green algae than in the entire space exploration program.[10] What I meant was that the value of science, like the value of art or literature, lies in its contribution to human understanding and that the value of a scientific project should be measured by the amount and breadth of new understanding it generates. What the space exploration program achieved in terms of scientific understanding was relatively little—a few facts of interest to geologists and astronomers but no new synthesis about the universe or the origin of life. Space exploration fulfilled the emotional wish of humankind to spring free from earthbound limitations. It enlarged our feeling of power over the forces of nature. It caught the imagination of the television-viewing public as a great musical comedy or a great football game might do. But it also added incentive to the fantasies of space wars not only in the minds of filmmakers but in those of our political leaders.

Science, in pursuing understanding, generates sources of power by making technologies possible. How the technologies are employed, their use or absence of use and the purposes of their use, is not in the hands of the scientists. It is in the hands of society—that is, of those groups of individuals who have or seek decision-making power in social affairs. In the case of the atom bomb, the physicists turned over to the government their skills in service of a grand new technology. And it was the government that made the decision to use the bomb—that is, it was society as represented more or less distantly by elected officials more familiar with the manipulation of power than with the process of understanding.

Technology can be constructive or destructive, depending on how it is used. For a few centuries we have reveled in optimism. For large segments of humankind, technology has meant steam power, and electricity, and cheap goods, and cleaner and healthier lives. It has been easy to ignore or to gloss over the negative effects, such as instability of employment, disruption of commercial structures, and colonial exploitation. Today, in a world living under an apparently permanent threat of nuclear war, the simple belief in beneficial technology has given way to widespread skepticism. Each scientific advance that can generate new technology is seen by many as a potential danger. Let us take as an example my own field, that of molecular biology. It has generated technologies with vast possibilities in applied biology. Genetic engineering, the methodology for reshuffling genes within and between organisms, promises new understanding of life processes, as well as new approaches to medicine and agriculture. We can visualize a whole range of applications, from production of cheap hormones to correction of certain congenital defects and to production of superior food plants.

This sounds wonderful, just as the electric motor or the cotton gin sounded wonderful one or two centuries ago. Yet, even before the first applications of genetic engineering become visible, we hear voices—some of them serious and thoughtful voices—warning us of dangers ahead: of possible accidents, of environmental catastrophes, of corruption of scientists if they become drawn into the service of industrial enterprise. And the consequences of genetic technology, we are told, may be more subtle than those of the construction of bombs or the alteration of the physical quality of life. These consequences may intrude into social relations at the level of mutual respect and social justice, as when eugenicists five decades ago preached the superiority of one human group over another or the inevitability of behavioral differences between sexes.

The misgivings extend not only to technology but to science itself. Since science is the source of technology, and technology can generate potentially dangerous applications, we hear critics say, Shouldn't science be limited, or constrained, or even stopped in its path? Isn't scientific research an altogether evil pursuit of power? Before we dismiss these criticisms and misgivings too lightly, we should realize that behind criticism of science as an enterprise is often a protest against the structure and functioning of society, a revulsion against injustice. There is a revulsion against social systems in which the fruits of science, like those of labor, are directed to selfish gain or private profit or to the preservation of power structures.

Every environmentalist, every critic of technology, is consciously or unconsciously something of a radical—that is, a person who questions the power relations within society. The central question radicals ask is, Who in society makes the decisions and in whose interest? Who calls the game and how is the deck stacked? Sorting out the rational and the irrational in scientific research may help protect the scientific enterprise from its radical critics. For example, the science of genetics has been the object of suspicion on the part of critics who see it as a source of racism and sexism. But what these critics have faulted is not the content of genetics; it is a superstructure of distortions advocated consciously or unconsciously by a few socially biased geneticists.

SCIENCE, TECHNOLOGY, AND THE QUESTION OF RESPONSIBILITY

The closer science moves to the problems of society, the more wary scientists should be of their own personal or class or sex biases. The danger of unwise applications may concern science itself less than science-derived technology. Yet, for scientists to dismiss the question of responsibility for the impact of science on society leaves them in an ambiguous position, somewhere between that of philosophers and poets on the one hand and that of handgun manufacturers on the other hand. At what point in the feedback loop of responsibility do its signals become irrelevant noise? Can we press indifferently any computer key without asking whether one of them may activate an electric chair or a nuclear warhead?

Awareness of the forces that operate in society becomes important. The ivory tower has windows for us to look out from as well as doors for delivery of knowledge. And what we see encourages, or rather compels, our participation. What form should such participation take?

We recognize the importance of scientists' informing the public of the advances of science so that when the public elects officials it can do so with better understanding of the landscape of available knowledge. And we recognize the importance of scientists' acting as advisors to such officials in the formulation of policy. But beyond such formal corporate service by scientists remains a serious question of responsibility to which science itself provides no answer.

The internal structure of science—its subject matter and mode of procedure—does not provide any answer. Science in principle deals with How come? and not with What for? Even the precious role of integrity within scientific research, the demand for open disclosure and reproducibility, is not so much a value as a necessary constraint. Science deals with good or bad theories and good or bad experiments, not with good or bad actions. The neutrality of science, however, ends at the intersection with technology. The "ceremony of innocence" stops here.

And yet, personal morality—the rules of behavior among individuals in day-to-day interactions—does not clearly prescribe any specific pattern of responsibility with regard to the social consequences of newly acquired knowledge. For thousands of years of Western philosophy, no one has come up with any better prescription than the Golden Rule, irrespective of how different philosophers have justified it. But what direction does the Golden Rule provide in a world of complex social and economic relations?

Economic realities introduce conflicts between personal morality and social ethics, conflicts that underlie the entire history of human society and become more acute in modern individualistic societies. Attempts to resolve such oppositions on a philosophical plane have obscured the essential conflict, between the individual drive to be virtuous and the drive to survive and prosper in a society where the supply of rewards is insufficient to satisfy all wants, let alone all desires.

Isaiah Berlin, the English philosopher, has expressed this dilemma in a provocative form, in terms of a Christian and a pagan ethical system—one personal, the other communal—struggling with one another within society.[11] Again, the ethicist Alasdair MacIntyre has suggested that our ethics is incoherent because it is a mosaic of ethical fragments of the past; it is composed of relics of principles that were functional in earlier societies with different forms of communal organization but that have now become dysfunctional.[12] According to MacIntyre, principles like the Golden Rule can be socially operational only in societies such as the hypothetical *polis* of Aristotle, in which citizens identify—at least formally—with a communal system of virtues. In individualistic modern society, the personal and communal systems of virtues are not congruent with each other. Competitive individualism interferes with the virtuous life of the community. Conflict reigns, or, to put it in MacIntyre's own words, politics becomes "civil war carried out with other means." What does this mean in terms of personal responsibility? Should we accept passively the divergence between personal morality and the chaotic values of our complex society?

What philosophers tell us is simply that the practice of the Golden Rule cannot be expected to prevail automatically in the affairs of society. If it is to become operative it must, like any other goal, be actively worked for. It must be an existentially chosen, actively nurtured prescription for relations among citizens just as for relations between individuals. In other words, it must become a *political goal*. An efficient ethics in society can come into being only when personal choices become political commitments, and individual commitments become collective commitments. The hope for a more just society where the output of science and all understanding is used for purposes collectively agreed upon—a society with true political legitimacy—must first become a political commitment on the part of individuals to make it become so.

Unfortunately, commitment to active political participation, especially at the national level, has been extremely rare in our country—in fact, more extremely so than in any of the other democracies. Little more than one half of the eligible voters register to vote, and little more than half of those registered cast their votes. Indifference to politics is compounded by skepticism about the political process and even contempt of politicians. The roots of this situation are deep and complex. They go back at least to the 1830s, when Jacksonian democracy converted the electoral process to a spoils system, destroying the sense of political community and communal commitment that had animated the Founding Fathers and their successors for half a century. Now more than ever our complex society requires commitment to communal goals on the part of its citizens.

Such a need for commitment to active political participation applies to scientists as well as to everyone else—more so, perhaps, because scientists are collectively the source of so much of the power that underlies modern technological society. Scientists more than other groups in society cannot look down on political life with indifference or contempt. Whatever their personal choices may be, whatever side they choose, their voices need to be heard. When intellectuals, the purveyors of understanding, exile themselves from the arena of social struggles and seek refuge in the ivory tower, they lose a significant part of their humanity. This does not mean that scientists should politicize science or philosophers politicize philosophy. On the contrary, politically committed scientists and philosophers should bring to the political arena the methods and integrity of their intellectual pursuits.

In the third canto of the *Inferno*, Dante relegates the souls of the uncommitted, who in life have deserved neither blame nor praise, to Limbo, where the punishment is to be forever among others like themselves. They have lived a politically passive life doing their chores but contributing nothing to the collective process of guiding and perfecting the community. Dante, the political poet, calls on us to be the artificers of the world we live in, not only by interpreting it, as in Wallace Stevens's poem, but by committing ourselves to active participation. There is nothing new in this way of looking at politics as social morality in action. Rousseau and other philosophers have seen the impossibility of living a moral life without active concern for the legitimacy of the surrounding society. If personal morality and social organization are to become more congruent, they will not do so automatically by any fatefully prescribed historical process. They will converge only as a result of deliberate, committed personal and collective activity. To think otherwise is to indulge in wishful thinking, not unlike a belief in astrology or in miracles.

Serving as political activists, or at least as committed citizens, is not as easy a task as following the pursuit of science and understanding in libraries or laboratories, and it offers little promise of short-range success and reward. But it is a task that provides reassurance against despair and reinforcement through shared purpose.

PANEL DISCUSSION

BRILL: Dr. Luria, do you think that scientists generally are more individualistic now, less socially responsible as a group, than they were in the 1960s or even before then? If so, what is going to change their attitudes?

LURIA: I would say that by and large the involvement of scientists in general affairs tends to be lower than that of other scholars. Scientists, because of the operation of their work, tend to be more concentrated in the kinds of things that can be put into a paradigm. For example, you can make a hypothesis and test it. In the world of politics you cannot operate like that. In society you operate by commitment; you have to choose what you like and what you believe, whether it is monetarism or socialism, and then act upon it without any way or expectation of testing by experiment whether you are right or wrong.

On the other hand, after the atom bomb, many physicists realized what their involvement already was, whether they liked it or not, and they became very active. Biologists have not yet because most of the applications of biology until now have really been extremely positive, and they continue to be. That is why I emphasize the fact that even about biology you now begin to hear critics worrying about where the future may take us.

KEVLES: There was a magnificent display of social responsibility on the part of molecular biologists and others in the Asilomar Conference in 1975, in which biologists who knew about these [developments in recombinant DNA] basically said: "Wait a minute; let's stop before we proceed with this science. Shouldn't we examine not only its technical implications but also our moral responsibilities with regard to taking this kind of risk for the rest of the world?" In the end it was decided that the risk was very minimal and could be taken. And to date, despite the fact that there has been enormous work in recombinant DNA all over the world, there have been so far as anybody knows no adverse consequences.

Now, the question that arises in my mind is this. In the early 1970s and certainly before, biologists could take the position of moral responsibility in a rather uniform way, partly because they had the precedent of nuclear scientists with Hiroshima but also because biologists were pretty much in the ivory tower at that time. Since then, however, molecular biology has gone far beyond and outside of the ivory tower. Biotechnological business has become enormously important financially and many biologists have taken on financial commitments and opportunities. Given that trend, can we expect biologists to exercise and display this same degree of social responsibility? That is, to what degree is the commercialization of biology affecting it?

LURIA: I do not see how the fact that biology has now become involved in areas of application with a range of financial reward is going to change the basic situation: that biologists, like chemists, like most physicists, and so on, live in a world that is different from the world in which what we call political decisions are made. By *political* I do not mean only, for example, to talk to the public and to discuss in public the possible dangers. I am putting it in harsh words now: there is in any society a need for the intellectual to boil over any sign of injustice. Revulsion against injustice is what is called for and nobody is more responsible for that than the people who have the privilege of living with intellectual pursuits.

NELSON: I hear it said quite often that the new interest in immediate commercialization and profit-taking in not only genetic science but others related to it is actually having very detrimental effects upon the integrity and the purity of scientific research with regard to the publication of results, a result of intense competition among scientists quickly to capitalize on a particular achievement. How true is that observation?

LURIA: Let me put it this way. Exactly ten years ago I wrote for a magazine called *Focus* an article that explained why scientists don't cheat. But of course the editor of the magazine, without asking me, put on the title "Why Do Scientists Cheat?" Now, what I mean is that there are two aspects to your question: you mentioned integrity and you mentioned competition. Competition, absolutely. But I think any human activity that is moving forward actively is bound to involve competitive people who are active, desirous to get results, and so on.

Integrity is very different. I think that contrary to what newspapers and science writers love to [print], if you were to scrutinize all activity, science and specifically the biological sciences have had the highest integrity of all the professions. I had a visit once from somebody who came to see me informally; we had a couple of drinks together at a bar. He happened to be an FBI agent and he told me, "You know, Doctor, we could send two-thirds of the Congress to jail tomorrow." Well, you could not send any measurable number of scientists to jail. The fact is that this is a profession in which, for better or for worse, integrity is built in. If you cheat on something that anybody will read within three months or six months, you will be caught. If you care to invent a completely irrelevant paper on some minor subspecies of algae that nobody's working on, very well, you may get it published, but I doubt it even today; even that will be sent to a good algologist who is going to say, "This is bunk." I think it is a profession on whose integrity I can stand any time with respect to that of lawyers, of real estate agents, or car salesmen.

BYRNE: You stated that creation and order result from human activity—that is, "music from the noise of nature." Would it not be more correct to say that human activity uncovers the order inherent in the universe?

LURIA: I think as always you can never write something or say something that someone else cannot say better. In fact, I must say I wrote a few sonnets in my life but Shakespeare always did it better before me. But let's comment on this. I think that is a very subtle point, the difference between whether it uncovers the order or whether it provides it. The point in the idea of order as formulated by Wallace Stevens in several poems and by many others is that until the human consciousness operates on reality, there is no such thing as an order because order only exists if it is recognized. Now, if God exists in a form that has consciousness over everything that exists in the universe, then this order already exists. But, apart from God, the human species is the only one that creates order by acting and by observing and by studying. So that, I think, is the distinction. Order is only meaningful for us because we put things together. I recommend to anybody who has not read *Ideas of Order* to read it; it's a marvelous book of poetry.*

KEVLES: Just a brief observation. I think that the issue really has to be understood to be moot, whether order exists in the universe or whether we impose order in the universe. There's no way to tell, no way at all.

LURIA: I am a Poparian realist. I am doubtful of possibilistic escapes.

SMITH: Well, I thought that one of the really interesting points that was made in this talk was the emphasis that Professor Luria placed on the idea of science or the enterprise of science as a social process, a process that deeply involves politics. But if you talk about the Golden Rule being actively worked for, getting people involved, pursuing political goals, it's possible that the enterprise of science would become more disorderly in a political sense than orderly. Any comments about that?

LURIA: I think that there are two ways of avoiding the possibility of trouble—one is to face it, and the other is to put one's head in the sand, hoping it will go away. It won't. I think that, in fact, science is too important to continue to be simultaneously

---

*In *The Collected Poems of Wallace Stevens* (New York: Alfred A. Knopf, 1955), 115–162.

protected and neglected benignly by society. I think we are too important not to be active parts of the process. I see a great advantage in biologists going in and creating their own industrial companies, not only because it is nice to know that our students can make money, but also because I think that this is going to give us a shelter [between] all science being in the hands of five or six multinational corporations, or science being closed in the laboratories. I think it puts a buffer between [these extremes]. It is a matter of initiative here. Biotechnology in a sense is creating a buffer between Monsanto and Dow Chemical, for instance, and science. I have worked enough for large companies as a consultant to know how much nicer life is in a small biotechnological company in which initiative is still close to the basic research.

KEVLES: You mentioned in your talk that science is fundamentally value free. It describes the way the world is, not the way it ought to be. But I think that on the point of view of our discussion at the moment, it's worth observing that the doing of science itself is not value free. It constitutes a deep assertion of a whole cluster of values. One could mention many of them. I'll only point, for example, to belief in intellectual freedom, which is fundamental to the doing of science; belief in and the necessity for rational knowledge, however any historical moment happens to define rationality. (I would disagree with you about alchemists; I don't think they were irrational in their own context.) It also, however, involves the assertion of social values as well, especially these days. It clearly involves demand for investment of enormous public resources. It involves a constraint on methods. You can't do just whatever you please in the doing of science. Take the simple case of human experimentation. There are severe restraints justifiably placed on those things. Knowledge itself, in short, does not transcend all other values. And then in contemporary science, many values express themselves in its social organization and management.

The basic conclusion that I would draw from these observations, by way of clarification of the argument you've been making, is that science is no longer at all autonomous in itself—that is, in the doing of science. It involves money. It involves resources. It is fundamentally an integral part of the larger society and it is misleading to speak of it as something that science does and then society uses. It is much more an interactive activity now between science and the larger society because science is itself a part—fundamentally, integrally—of the larger society itself.

LURIA: What I meant is that the *content* of science is value free, but that the *process* of science is anything but value free. For example, I wrote in my own autobiography that one of the reasons I wanted to go into science (looking back at myself with a slightly psychoanalytic eye) was that I wanted to escape from the social world in which I had been raised and I was impressed by how my young friends who were the sons of scientists seemed to be so much happier.* That was my first motivation. So, you see, it's anything but value free. But if you are a good scientist, the way you proceed in the operation of science depends on the content. Really, there is a duality. The content of science does not dictate values, but the way science is performed is permeated with the same values.

KEVLES: Hence, you have got to expect some kind of governance and regulation imposed on science from the outside society. That is inevitable.

LURIA: You had better be in politics, then, so you can take part in that.

NOTES

1. *The Collected Poems of Wallace Stevens* (New York: Alfred A. Knopf, 1955), 128.
2. Ibid., 129.
3. Herbert Marcuse, *An Essay on Liberation* (Boston: Beacon Press, 1969), 40.
4. R. D. Laing, *The Divided Self* (New York: Pantheon Books, 1969).
5. Jerry Adler et al., "James Watt's Land Rush," *Newsweek* 29 (June 1981): 29. U.S. Congress. House. Committee on Interior and Insular Affairs. *Briefing by the Secretary of the Interior.* 97th Cong. 1st sess., 1981, p. 37.
6. *New York Times,* March 16, 1981: 16; *New York Times,* July 22, 1981: 20.
7. *New York Times,* Jan. 6, 1982: 1; *New York Times,* Nov. 23, 1982: 23.
8. Samuel Beckett, *The Lost Ones* (New York: Grove Press, 1972).
9. P. B. Medawar, *The Art of the Soluble* (New York: Barnes and Noble, 1969). See also Medawar, *Pluto's Republic: Incorporating "The Art of the Soluble" and "Induction and Intuition in Scientific Thought"* (New York: Oxford University Press, 1982).

---

*S. E. Luria, *A Slot Machine, A Broken Test Tube: An Autobiography* (New York: Harper & Row, 1984).

10. *New York Times,* Oct. 5, 1975, VI: 73.
11. Isaiah Berlin. *Against the Current: Essays in the History of Ideas* (New York: Viking Press, 1980), 53–54.
12. Alasdair MacIntyre, *After Virtue: A Study in Moral Theology* (Notre Dame: University of Notre Dame Press, 1981).

4. The Impact of Biotechnology and the Future of Agriculture

WINSTON J. BRILL

My purpose in this paper is twofold: to convince you that bio-technological research is opening up exciting new approaches for improvements in agriculture, and to put into perspective the concerns about safety that have surfaced regarding these new methods. The technology in question is genetic engineering, a technique by which one extracts a segment of a chromosome, purifies it, and splices it into a different organism. Also called gene splicing, the method is only a little more than a decade old. While it is now possible to put genes into only a few kinds of organisms, the number of organisms becoming amenable to this technology is increasing significantly. For researchers such as I, the technique holds enormous promise for agriculture, but with the promise come potential pitfalls that critics have noted, occasionally with raised voices. This paper explores both the promises and pitfalls of biotechnology and the future of agriculture.

Over the past ten years or so, we have come to know much more about our world thanks to genetic engineering. We are learning how organisms evolve by examining purified genes. We are learning more about the basis of cell development. We are learning about diseases and their relationships to micro-organisms that cause them. We are learning how some cancers and viruses work. All of this knowledge has accrued due to the work of researchers engaged in genetic engineering: it is a very exciting field.

And interestingly enough, the technology involved is not extraordinarily sophisticated. High schools are becoming increasingly involved in the study of recombinant DNA and gene splicing.

Laboratories in developing countries are involved in genetic engineering. Major universities throughout the world house laboratories engaged in this field, and of course numerous industries have become involved. There is even, I have recently heard, a home genetic engineering kit on the market. So the genie is out of the bottle, and it is impossible to put it back.

From the perspective of biology, one important aspect of this growing technology is its commercial application. Consider, for example, the health care field, toward which most of the applications have been directed so far. The production of the hormone insulin is a case in point. Diabetics require daily doses of insulin, which normally is extracted from the pancreas of a slaughterhouse cow or sheep. Certain diabetics, however, develop reactions or allergies to these animal insulins, yet the number of human pancreases available to produce human insulin is small. Scientists now have isolated the gene for insulin

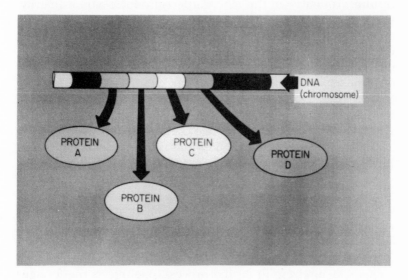

The rod represents a chromosome, which is composed of DNA. A chromosome is segmented into genes, each of which codes for a different protein. A living cell contains thousands of genes. The genetic engineer seeks to isolate a gene and "splice" it into a chromosome in a different living organism.

from human cells, have put that gene into a bacterium, and have grown the microorganism in a fermenter, rather like the type used in the brewing industry. The microorganism grows in this vat full of nutrients. In addition to its other genes, the microorganism contains the new gene, which results in its producing human insulin. When the cells in the vat have finished growing, the laboratory harvests the material and purifies the human insulin. The end product can be pounds of insulin exactly equivalent to the insulin produced in a normal human body. At present, Eli Lilly and Company markets this product under the name Humulin, and it is only one of a number of proteins now being produced in this manner.

In terms of agricultural applications, many of the early developments applied to animal health care are a direct outgrowth of the work done in human health. The production of bovine interferon closely approximates the process just described for insulin. Animals—in this case, cattle—produce extraordinarily small amounts of interferon, so little, in fact, that to purify enough to do substantial research with it has been impossible. Genetic engineering efforts, however, have produced bovine interferon in quantities sufficient to run experiments testing interferon as a possible protective agent against shipping fever, a commercially important disease. Another example occurs with vaccines, such as the one that prevents pig scours, a disease that afflicts baby pigs. Efforts are now under way to produce an effective vaccine to combat foot-and-mouth disease in cattle. Bovine growth hormone is another protein that appears in small amounts in nature but that genetic engineers have made in quantity in the laboratory. Tested at Cornell University, this substance has produced substantially faster growth in cattle, which, in turn, have produced 30 to 40 percent more milk than cattle not treated with the hormone.

In some cases researchers have genetically engineered the animals themselves. To do the process, one injects the foreign gene for growth hormone, for instance, directly into a freshly fertilized embryo and implants the embryo into a female, which then gives birth to the genetically engineered offspring. The process is not down to an art as yet; it is tremendously complicated. In many cases the offspring are sterile, and yet, some

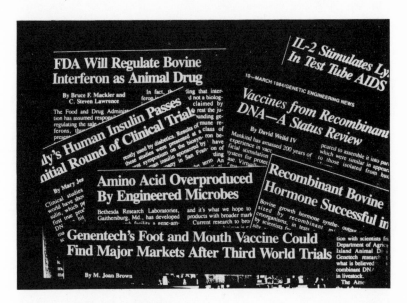

These headlines indicate the variety of areas in which genetic engineers are currently researching.

successes have occurred in which the animals are fertile and their progeny retain the foreign gene. The United States Department of Agriculture has genetically engineered pigs and sheep in this manner, although data on the size and growth of the animals are not in yet.

These experiments have raised questions in some quarters. Consider, for example, that faster-growing animals require more feed. We may therefore be inadvertently giving a competitive advantage to milk producers whose cattle are close to feed-growing areas, as opposed to producers who must ship in feed. In Australia, where efforts to genetically engineer larger sheep are in process, concerns exist that the larger sheep will increase the strain on a very fragile environment by compacting the soil more and thus increasing erosion.

These objections to genetic engineering, however, need to be put in perspective. We have traditionally bred farm animals and applied nutritional science in order to increase their weight and

This cartoon, "The Cow Pock—or—the Wonderful Effects of the New Inoculation!" from c. 1800, satirizes Edward Jenner's efforts to inoculate against smallpox with a vaccine taken from diseased cattle.

their rate of growth. The end product is the same, whether achieved through genetic engineering or through more traditional means. Some concerns exist that this technology ought not to occur because it is unnatural, that only through the human intervention of genetic engineering is the growth of these animals made possible. Granted. But the animals we know today, be they farm animals or pets, are themselves the product of human intervention in the areas of breeding and nutrition. The point, then, is *not* whether human intervention will occur, but whether or not we will apply the knowledge we are gaining through genetic engineering to this area of humankind's endeavors.

New technologies have long generated skepticism and outright opposition. Cartoonists satirized Edward Jenner's attempts to vaccinate the people of England against smallpox in 1800. One particular cartoon showed a person, vaccinated with the pus from an infected cow, erupting in miniature cows all over his body. Jenner endured ridicule and was almost dismissed by medical society because he suggested a course of action that people thought was unnatural. Yet, because of Jenner's vaccine, a disease that accounted at one time for the deaths of approximately 30 percent of English infants is all but unheard of today. Technologies once branded "unnatural" by society have, as in this case, sometimes produced remarkable medical and social good.

Agricultural applications of genetic engineering have not been restricted only to the world of farm animals. Genetically engineered plants are the subject of much research, too, including my own and that of my company. The process of genetically engineering plants is similar to that used directly to engineer animals. In other words, one can add a foreign gene to a single cell isolated from, say, a leaf, which then is incorporated among the tens of thousands of genes in the cell. Given certain nutrients and hormones, the cell will grow into a normal, fertile plant whose seeds contain the foreign gene, thus transferring the gene from generation to generation. Researchers are using this technique to produce plants that are resistant to diseases, that have improved nutritional quality, and that are more resistant to drought, among other properties. Some researchers are seeking to develop plants that require less applied fertilizer, since fertilizer is a major source of pollution when it runs off into streams and rivers. The genetic engineering of plants is in its early stages of development, but this increasingly active area promises exciting applied results over the next decades.

These discoveries will and do originate in laboratories, but a very important step in the process when applied to agriculture is field-testing. It needs to be done as soon as possible. The reason for this need for haste is that even in the best of greenhouses we cannot mimic, cannot even closely approximate, all the environmental activities that a plant experiences out in nature. It is crucial that plants or microorganisms go out into the field before one expends great sums of time, effort, and money refining a plant for greenhouse conditions, only to discover that the process does not work in the field.

Field-testing genetically engineered plants has caused concern that has not applied to other uses of the method. No one has objected to the production of insulin, because it is contained by the fermenter. Nor am I aware of concerns that genetically engineered cows are put out in the field. But people are concerned about putting plants and microorganisms out in the field. Discussions of this issue are sometimes marked by rationality, and sometimes not. These concerns, in my opinion, are mostly due to fear of the unknown.

I recall a cartoon in which a politician asserts, "Not only am I against evolution, but I'm not so sure about gravity and relativity either." My point is not to denigrate politicians. What has happened, I wish to suggest, is that some of the more vocal concerned people have triggered a response among politicians, some of whom have neither the background nor the patience to hear all sides of the argument. In other words, at least some politicians only need to hear that field-testing could be "dangerous" to call for hearings that may result in regulations or laws restricting field-testing. Such regulations may not eventually benefit society. It is essential, therefore, that people involved in this area talk to politicians and their aides in order to educate them on these issues and to ensure that irrationality does not carry the day.

My point of view is that field-testing these plants and microorganisms ought to cause no special concern. I will make my argument through a comparison of traditional agricultural practice with what might occur from a plant-genetic or microgenetic engineering experiment.

Teosinte, presumed by some to be the progenitor of corn, grows wild in Central America. It would not cross naturally with the corn grown today in the American Midwest, but scientists around the world are trying to breed characteristics from teosinte into corn. Teosinte has disease resistances, for example, that we would like to have in corn. Other scientists have for decades been crossing other crop plants and exotic species, such as tomatoes and little black berries that you might never guess are a relative of the tomato, to improve crops.

With traditional methods, when one crosses corn with teosinte the genes are mixed up randomly, so that the researcher cannot predict what the progeny will look like until the experiment is done. All the progeny are different from one another. In a genetic engineering experiment, however, the scientist takes a very specific gene from a related organism and splices it into a cell. The scientist, having isolated the gene and knowing its function, can predict what the progeny will look like. Predictability, in fact, is the purpose of the experiment.

Now, in the case of crosses, breeders take no precautions, even though a critic might argue that a cross might produce some very terrible weed. Breeders are not concerned because, after decades of experience with innumerable crosses done in

"Not only am I against evolution but I'm not so sure
about gravity and relativity, either."

Issues related to genetic engineering have political repercussions. Unlike the candidate in the cartoon above, politicians must be open to discussion of scientific uses with specialists as well as with the general public. *(S. Harris)*

many countries by sophisticated and not-so-sophisticated researchers alike, no serious problems have occurred. Nothing so serious as to frighten us has happened. Breeding has produced some minor problems, to be sure, and so will genetic engineering. Occasionally, plants bred for resistance to a disease prove susceptible to another disease, an unintended consequence of the experiment. Problems of this sort have happened and will continue to happen; the breeder's profession, in fact, is to look for these problems. And so breeders field-test with both small and large plots. Genetic engineering, we can expect, will confront problems of a similar magnitude and no larger. No cause seems to exist, therefore, for regulations for this method as it presents no special concerns and as we see no need for special regulations to control breeding of plants.

Critics have charged that special concerns exist. Their models of what might happen with the genetic engineering of plants include the devastation caused by the Japanese beetle, Dutch elm disease transmitted by the elm bark beetle, the waterways in the South clogged by hydrilla, forests ravaged by the gypsy moth, and Southern trees choked by the kudzu vine. These organisms have indeed wreaked havoc. The fact is, however, that these organisms are not problems because humankind has genetically manipulated them. They became problems because, as is true of almost every crop and ornamental plant now grown in the United States, they were imported from another country. Most imported plants have been valuable; the ones that have caused serious problems are exceptional. But the key to the problem has been importation. In their native lands these organisms had evolved over eons to be competitive, which is why they survived. They did not take over in those environments, though, because natural limiting factors—such as other plants, weather, and pathogens—existed. The problems arose only when one or more of the natural limiting factors were removed, as happened in the importation of these particular organisms.

Absolutely no scientific basis exists to believe that by genetically engineering corn, wheat, or rice one could inadvertently produce a serious problem weed. Serious problem weeds are not the result of a change in a single gene. They must in general terms meet a variety of criteria. The seed, for instance, would need to survive for a long time; it might have to be dispersed over a great distance; the plant would have to grow faster and be more vigorous than the plants around it. These properties are not produced by one gene, but by hundreds if not thousands of genes. The presence of certain genes is not sufficient, either, to produce a problem weed, for these must then interact in a very orderly, specific fashion. How could one imagine that by engineering one or even several genes in an organism, corn might be converted into a problem weed? The chance of producing a problem weed through this technique is less than the chance of producing one through a traditional cross of corn and teosinte. And no one is concerned about the latter.

Fortunately, debates on this issue have reduced anxiety about putting genetically engineered plants out into the environment. The same cannot be said for microorganisms that have been genetically engineered. Microorganisms are invisible; they have been known to cause disease; therefore, people who have had no experience in microbiology naturally can be somewhat worried.

This issue, too, requires perspective. A brochure distributed by the National Nitro-Culture Company of Pennsylvania advertised bacteria specifically for alfalfa that it claimed to be "the greatest discovery of the century." Printed in 1904, the brochure's claim was rather modest, but the point is that farmers have added microbes to their fields since the turn of the century. Over the years microorganisms have dramatically benefited the production of alfalfa, soybeans, and clover, among other crops. Since the turn of the century companies have produced hundreds of microbial inoculants, and farmers have regularly applied on the order of a billion microbes per acre. The use of microorganisms is not a new practice. It is an established practice and it is widespread.

One can imagine, furthermore, that for the hundreds of microbial products used commercially, ten or perhaps one hundred times more have been used experimentally. In the past eighty years in the United States (not to mention in India and the Soviet Union, whose production exceeds that of America), companies have grown billions of microbes in fermenters and farmers have applied them to their fields. In many cases those microorganisms were mutated, and yet in no case did a microbe

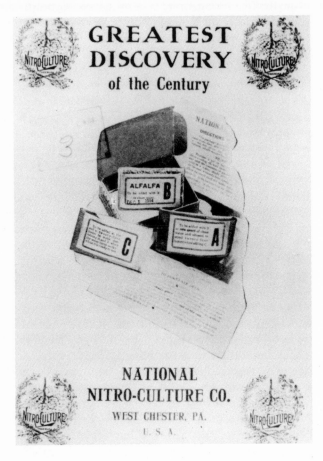

Advertisement issued by the National Nitro-Culture Co. in 1904. Microbial inoculants have been used in agriculture since the turn of the century.

cause a problem. Microbes do not represent a threat to humankind simply because they are microbes.

Genetic engineering can in fact improve microbial inoculants. Rhizobium has been used commercially in the Midwest for more than a decade to improve soybean production. The organism can be isolated and genetically manipulated so that it does better what it normally does, which is to fix nitrogen. Plants treated with this Rhizobium fix more nitrogen and thus are more vigorous. Genetic engineering, then, can be used to improve already useful organisms.

Criticisms persist. A major source of anxiety is that genetic engineering will produce a problem pathogen—that is, one that could spread readily and cause grief by infecting animals, or plants, or humans. The chance of such an occurrence is extraordinarily low. The situation is parallel to that of problem weeds: a pathogenic microorganism is *not* simply the result of a single gene. Studies of microbial ecology and the molecular basis of pathogenesis have shown that pathogens are the result of a complex of very specific genes interacting in well-tuned ways. For example, a pathogen may contain a gene for a toxin, but this gene is not in itself sufficient to make the organism pathogenic. The organism may also need one or more genes to overcome host defense mechanisms, or other genes to survive in between hosts. A leading molecular biologist of pathogenesis, in fact, claims that even with the many resources available to him he could not purposely convert a "safe" organism into a problem pathogen. So the prospect of accidentally producing a pathogen while trying to engineer an agriculturally useful organism is extremely small. This matter simply does not merit extensive concern.

Even in nature, microorganisms exchange genetic material, but in a purely random fashion. Consider that an average cubic inch of soil is composed of twenty million cells—microorganisms—that are continually dividing, mutating, and exchanging genetic matter with related organisms. More and more evidence suggests that exchanges occur between unrelated organisms, between plants and bacteria, for example. In most cases in which a bacterium has taken up a plant gene the exchange does not give the bacterium a selective advantage and the organism does not predominate. In rare cases a selective advantage does result, and the organism can predominate; we call that eventuality evolution. In any case, the negative impact that might result from genetic engineering of microorganisms is minuscule and insignificant when compared to the impact of the random exchanges that occur naturally.

Concerns about the safety of genetic engineering persist, in spite of the fact that the technology is at least as safe as traditional genetic techniques. *("The Far Side" cartoon by Gary Larson is reprinted by permission of Chronicle Features, San Francisco.)*

Recent events surely have fueled the controversy over gene-splicing technology, and print and electronic media have given considerable attention to these matters. The accidents at Love Canal and Three Mile Island, and the recent disaster at the Union Carbide plant in Bhopal are often treated as models of what might happen with recombinant DNA experiments. The builders of the Bhopal plant asserted that their factory was safe, moreover, just as I am claiming that the technology in my industry is safe. But the analogies are seriously flawed. The three specific instances just mentioned each involved a dangerous chemical, including the radioactive chemicals at Three Mile Island. At Bhopal, the chemical in question was methyl isocyanate, which everyone would and did agree was dangerous. Great potential for hazard exists in producing methyl isocyanate, in using it, in storing it, in disposing of it, and in transporting it. An accident involving a truck carrying methyl isocyanate and another vehicle would be a very serious problem. No such danger can arise from a recombinant organism, even by the fermenterful or the truckload. The situations are considerably different.

Before one gets excessively worried about putting genetically altered organisms into the environment, moreover, one ought to consider the current dangers that follow from the use of pesticides. Most of the genetic engineering being done in agriculture, ironically enough, is aimed at reducing present-day health hazards. Not only are the risks smaller with genetic engineering, but successfully applied, the technology will reduce the present reliance on pesticides and solve problems that pesticides do not.

Twenty percent of the farmers in Illinois, according to a recent study, have consulted a physician at least once with an ailment related to the use of pesticides. More and more data accumulate that show that pesticides get into the human food supply and thus into us. Evidence indicates that at least some of these pesticides are potentially carcinogenic. Over time, four hundred species of agricultural pests have grown resistant to insecticides and herbicides, reducing the effectiveness of these chemicals. In soil treated with herbicide, furthermore, microorganisms mutate in order to degrade the herbicide. As a result, the farmer either cannot use the herbicide the following year or must use more of it. The organisms—insecticide-resistant insects, herbicide-degrading bacteria, herbicide-resistant weeds—disseminate by natural means and exchange genes with other organisms. Therefore, the use of pesticides results in uncharacterized genetic changes in problem organisms; the use of genetic engineering results in characterized genetic changes in safe organisms. Once again, the difference is noteworthy.

The middle of the 1980s is a crucial and exciting time to be involved in genetic engineering related to agriculture. It is crucial because emerging regulations will at least temporarily resolve the debates over the safety of the technique and of field-testing. My belief is that the chance of producing a problem organism through recombinant DNA technology is less than the chance of doing so through practices that we now accept and manage. My hope is that as regulations evolve from discussions within and among the Environmental Protection Agency, the United States Department of Agriculture, the Food and Drug Administration, and the National Institutes of Health, rational arguments will prevail. The decision-making bodies must listen to these arguments as put forth by scientists, by public advocacy groups, by environmentalists, and others, and should not be led by those vivid imaginings that any new technology inspires.

It is an exciting time because gene-splicing technology is at an early stage. We are beginning to use its first products. My prediction is that our future will be considerably improved by this technology, and that in the process this technology will prove safer than the one it will displace. In a manner of speaking, it is "back to nature."

PANEL DISCUSSION

BYRNE: Winston, how do you account for the concern on the part of ecologists (many of whom have a considerable number of degrees in microbiology, it seems to me) who persist in not accepting your argument? They suggest that in fact there are dangers here. Maybe it comes down to the danger of, as one of my colleagues put it, What if you're wrong?

BRILL: It's not a matter of genetic engineers versus ecologists. There are a few ecologists, probably no more than a handful that I know of, who have expressed concern. I know many more than a handful who are not concerned. They're interested; they're not afraid; they have the same kind of sense that I have. There are also some recombinant DNA people who have expressed concern, but they are in the minority. So it's not ecologists versus molecular biologists at all. Basically, the ecologists who have expressed concern have been studying some of these upsetting things—starlings, gypsy moths, and so on. What they have been focusing on for most of their careers have been problems that can occur from a live organism. They are very sensitive to that and we definitely need that population. That's basically it.

What if I'm wrong? Anybody can say that about any technology. I'm quoting other people now, but we inject our children with millions of doses of certain vaccines and some people have said, Well, how do we know that with those vaccines we're not also including some virus or agent that will cause cancers, perhaps even cancers that will only appear twenty years from now? As we've had more and more experience with these vaccines we can't say we know absolutely that they are safe. But based on our experiments and our best estimates at this time, we feel that we are safe and we're doing some very important things for people.

The disadvantage we have in arguing the case, especially with politicians, is that they are sensitized to that question, What if you're wrong? That's where it stops, and they really don't have the patience to listen to the arguments. We have had experience with recombinant DNA technology for over a decade. Certainly, laboratory organisms have gotten out into the environment; probably millions of different kinds of laboratory organisms have. Just a little droplet that can contain hundreds of thousands of organisms can get into your shoe or on your hand and you go out into the environment. So we do have some experience with recombinant DNA technology in all kinds of organisms, and, more important, we have experiences with the more traditional practices. Recombinant DNA isn't going to change organisms radically, or if it does change the organism radically, it will become a dead organism.

KEVLES: Apropos your last point, my understanding was that in the case of microorganisms of recombinant DNA, at least in the beginning, a strain of *E. coli* was used that was known not to have a tremendous chance of survival outside the laboratory environment. It seems to me the case with plants is different. You want them to survive outside the laboratory environment, for openers. But it would seem to me that it would be difficult to predict, given their survivability outside the laboratory, just what impact they might have on the overall ecological balance of the given environment. I am curious to know, first of all, how you actually assess that in a concrete case. Second, how do you think decisions about whether genetically engineered plants ought to be released into the environment should be made? Where should the nexus of power and authority in society lie? Should it lie with you folks entirely or us or whom?

BRILL: Well, the first question is really how does one assess what the potential for problems will be with a plant that you have genetically engineered, presumably to do something useful. It's no different from the traditional practice, which is the business of the plant breeder, who takes a plant and runs a small plot and compares that to the best plant around, to its controls. In fact, sometimes it takes a decade because breeders first try a new plant that comes from a teosinte cross or two different varieties of corn in a small plot and hopefully they see something that makes it better. Then, they try it over many seasons, over many environments. And really that's the experience they get. Sometimes, mistakes are made and a plant becomes a commercial plant and it turns out to be susceptible to a major disease. There was a corn blight in 1970 that caused havoc in the Midwest, but that was easily overcome. I mean it was an economic problem for a year but there was nothing ecological, really.

In fact, it's the growing of the crops that does something ecologically. It changes the types of insects that hang around these crops, the kinds of microbes that hang around the crops. That is accepted and no problems have occurred from that practice. Similarly, I think, because genetic engineering is going to make even less of a change in the plant, the chance for anything unexpected to happen is going to be much less. So it is a testing that agricultural communities have been involved with for many decades; all state universities have extension programs and farms to look at some of the new varieties. That's the traditional way and perhaps the only way. There has been some talk about coming out with a laboratory test to see if organism X has potential for causing problems. While that would be very desirable, I think we're decades and decades away from that.

SMITH: There's a question in my mind about the economics

and sociology of the new techniques. Do you see these new technologies as accelerating the demise of the traditional family farm, or will they be equally available to everyone? What sort of economic and sociological effects would these techniques have? BRILL: I'm not an expert in this area, but there's a lot of discussion going on here, especially concerning cattle and growth hormones. There are predictions that indeed the technology will replace the small farmer. There is no question that agriculture will change. It will change with or without genetic engineering. I think that is really all I can say.

I know there are people involved in looking at the impact of these issues. Certainly, since the big companies are very much involved and they are after the money of the major farmers, I think it will be basically directed towards the big farmer. But you can look at it another way and say that it may be useful for the small farmer because one problem a small farmer has is purchasing pesticides and chemicals. Hopefully the plants and microorganisms that will be generated will decrease the need for these materials. So I think it's complex and I can't give you a proper answer.

Let me answer Dan's second question. Who should make the decisions? First of all, there are no regulations that govern these industries and there are a number of industries that have the opportunity to put genetically engineered organisms out into the environment. Every industry has tried to comply with the NIH's recombinant DNA guidelines. The decisions should be made by everybody being involved, really. So it should be the economists and the regulatory agencies and the industries and the scientists. It should be based on knowledge, not one person going off half-cocked, which is my biggest concern.
LURIA: I just wanted to reinforce something that Dr. Brill said that I don't think is often understood by the public or certainly by the newspapers. What one aims to do in genetic engineering, whether applied to animal husbandry or to plant breeding or to protection against diseases, is in a sense much more selective and precise than what you do, for example, when you breed two varieties in order to select the more resistant to diseases and so on. What you're trying to do, and what you can do, is to bring in one gene—that is, the one that interests you—with

a minimum amount of complication to the genetic structure as a whole. The less extraneous genetic material you bring, the more sure you are that you have only affected the characteristic. I would feel in principle much safer in using material that has been produced in this way than in trying, for example, to breed varieties of animals, as has been done for hundreds and thousands of years, in order to find one that is more suitable. We know of many cases where this has happened to sheep and so on, in which people have rushed to put hybrids into the field much too soon. In this case I think one has at least the confidence that the minimum amount of genetic reassortment has been accomplished.

NELSON: I want to raise a question that is also sociological, economic, and political. In the slide you showed of headlines from newspapers, I was struck by the headline that says, "Genentech Foot-and-Mouth Vaccine Could Find Major Markets After Third World Trials." I was puzzled about the Third World here. Does that mean because that is where the foot-and-mouth disease is found? (That is, outside the U.S. Congress, where it is often referred to!) But is it only in the Third World where this is a problem? If so, then the headline would be unexceptionable, I think. However, I've heard it often said by various critics that companies in the U.S. are more likely to go to Africa, South America, or Asia to try out their products—whether they be pharmaceuticals or any other genetically engineered products—in order to see whether they work because in this country the FDA or the EPA or the other agencies won't allow them to trial here. Now, is that a real problem in agricultural genetics?

BRILL: Well, I can't really speak for Genentech. First of all, [foot-and-mouth disease] is not a problem in the United States, but it is a problem in many other countries of the world. It's a disease that can spread readily, so it is a concern in the U.S. There is a special island off the East Coast called Plum Island that is the only place in the country where research of foot-and-mouth disease can occur, where they are working on the organism because they want to have a vaccine available should it come into the United States. So the incentives are both within the country and outside of the country. Europe, I think, is also very concerned about the foot-and-mouth disease and I think there have been some major outbreaks.

As to the matter of testing in Third World countries, this is a slightly different issue. First of all, these vaccines made through recombinant DNA either are not going to work or, if they work, should be totally safe because there is no chance of getting a disease from it (except for a potential allergic reaction) as you do with vaccines that are currently used. In fact, that's one of the beauties of some of the vaccines that are made through recombinant DNA, where all you inject into an animal or person is a single protein, whereas it will replace a vaccine where what you inject is a virus that is either killed in some manner or has been mutated so it is not virulent. There have been a number of cases where these have not been perfect, where people have been killed by virus vaccines that have not been totally killed or that have reverted into something pathogenic.

LURIA: The question that I'd like to raise now is very important. The fact is that the rules for putting materials on the market in the United States are fortunately the strictest in any country, except possibly Switzerland. But it has nothing to do with genetic engineering. Our large pharmaceutical companies have always tried their new drugs in countries that have more lax regulations before putting them on the market in this country. The recent scandal of Oraflex is only the most recent part of a long story in which companies do trials wherever they are allowed to do trials. That's somewhat due to the fact that the large companies have a power that goes, in a sense, beyond the wisdom of governments. And they can do this because there are other parts of the world in which governments do not protect their people as ours tries to.

BYRNE: Do you see potential military abuses of recombinant DNA research, say, in bacteriological or chemical warfare?

BRILL: There have been quite a few discussions on that. In fact, I went to the State Department a couple of years ago to listen to a debate on that topic. My belief is that if one wants to get involved in germ warfare, a whole lot of germs out there are readily available and one doesn't have to use recombinant DNA technology. As I said in my talk, I think it's going to be extremely difficult to make an organism worse than any organism we now have.

Some articles in the *Wall Street Journal* reported that Russia has an active germ warfare program using recombinant DNA, or at least their laboratories are into this. That has not been substantiated and I don't predict success. I've heard, for instance, that they are trying to put a very bad toxin gene into a microorganism. There are reasons to believe that if one did so the microorganism would not simply grow and multiply in the environment and be very prevalent. What it would do is die very quickly. So it's easier just to spray the toxin than the microorganism with the toxin.

The activity that is going on seems to be defensive. In other words, countries are asking what another country might do. What these countries might do may *not* involve genetic engineering. For instance, if somebody wants to spray a toxin around, there may be a vaccine produced here against that toxin. People are talking about that. But I can't imagine using genetic engineering to make an organism worse than any organism I can get right now.

5. Mechanistic Mischief and Dualistic Dangers in a Scientific Society

J. ROBERT NELSON

If the wording of my title seems obscure to you, please do not feel disturbed. It *is* obscure: not only to you and to a great many right-thinking citizens, but also to me. To tell the truth, I do not know how many people in this scientific society of ours are consciously committed to a mechanistic, materialistic view of human identity or human nature. Neither do I know how many thoroughgoing dualists there are, especially those who believe that the true essence of humanhood is spirit or soul, while the material nature of a person is not only finite but evil as well. Moreover, I am neither wise enough nor well enough informed to know all the implications of mechanistic material-ism or of anthropological dualism. I cannot doubt that among my very distinguished colleagues of the conference are persons who understand mechanism and dualism better than I do. In fact, they are probably identified with one or the other, in which case they may not at all be pleased with the pejorative nouns I have used to describe their views: *mischief* and *dangers*.

Those are contentious words, of course. Even before defining what is meant by mechanism and dualism, I am using the title to resist and oppose them. Why should this be? I try not to be contentious, much less polemical, about other people's opinions, philosophical commitments, or articles of faith. An attitude of tolerance and irenic fairness is usually much more commenda-ble. The motto "live and let live" has as its corollary "think and let think." Especially calm equanimity is needed when we ex-press our views in the context of the realm of science.

We may like to believe the familiar characterizations of science as purely disinterested, free of ideological or religious encumbrances, unaffected by value-laden concepts or moral principles. After all, does it make any difference to the nature of a micro-biologist's research, or that of a physicist or a botanist, whether he or she espouses a certain philosophy about reality in general or humanity in particular? The biologist may be a scientific materialist, the physicist a sincere Lutheran, the botanist an unperturbed agnostic who simply loves green plants. But each can be a first-rate researcher and teacher in his or her special field. So who is concerned?

Yet, my title disrupts that calm and tolerant assumption by making negative prejudgments about two classes of thinking and philosophy, two kinds of *weltanschauung*. It charges that mechanists are mischievous and dualists are dangerous in our manifestly scientific North American society. This paper can demonstrate one of the following: either the prejudgment is warranted; or it is unwarranted; or, warranted or not, it does not matter very much to us.

Let me qualify what I mean by the two world views by applying adjectives. The one is thus *materialistic* mechanism; the other *anthropological* or *human* dualism.

MECHANISTIC MISCHIEF

To introduce the consideration of materialistic mechanism, let me draw your attention to the most obvious and visible achievement of many of its adherents. This is science-based technology. It is the most pervasive characteristic in American culture today, as well as in Western Europe and Japan.[1] How we could live today without the countless technological devices on which we depend is beyond imagining. Certainly, the volume of production of machines, gadgets, and synthetic materials is far greater than we need for decent and agreeable living. Yet, who can say for sure what an adequate volume would be—and what possible effect upon manufacturing, commerce, and consumer habits would such a judgment have? Ours *is* a scientific society and a technological culture. The basic discoveries, applications, inventions, and production have multiplied manyfold in the past forty years. And, technologically speaking, in the words of Ronald Reagan, "You ain't seen nothin' yet."

The point of mentioning this utterly familiar phenomenon is to remind you of two sides of scientific technology: the back and the front, so to speak; or better, the philosophical presupposition and the pathological consequence. The *presupposition* is the widely held, but not universally affirmed, belief that materialism and its mechanistic view of all things provide the most appropriate world view of scientists and engineers.[2] The pathological consequence of modern technology is the damaging of some human qualities necessary to authentic personhood. We need to look critically at each of these dimensions of technology.

There is a popular, cheapened use of the word *materialism* with which we can quickly dispense. It refers to our inordinate use of material products and possessions. It means that the consumer's appetite is insatiable; that the madness of pre-Christmas shopping or the frenzy of buying at the airport's duty-free shop is an acceptable symbol and index of human acquisitiveness. This referent of the word *materialism* indicates a very serious problem of human values; but it is not the problem now at hand.

Materialism as a pervading philosophy or world view goes deeper than consumerism. Some call it scientific materialism; others, mechanistic materialism; Marxists speak of a dialectical materialism as a total philosophy.[3] Whichever the adjective and the variable meaning, these have in common the one basic belief that everything in nature, everything in the world and cosmos, consists only of atoms. Atoms, constituted of electrical charges, are the substance of all matter. Molecules are structures of atoms; so molecules, joined together and arranged mechanically in varying scales of complexity, manifest all material things as mechanisms, whether inert or living. These are the data as well as the theories of atomism, materialism, and mechanism.

That this view of reality has commended itself to experimental scientists is quite understandable. It allows no undetectable, invisible, unquantifiable factor to taunt the sensory faculties of human subjects. In former centuries it fortunately served to emancipate scientists from superstition and magic. In the past century materialism has enabled scientists to conceptualize the patterns and interactions of innumerable structures of physical matter, both inert and organic. Indeed, scientists' findings in research have often led them either, first, to adopt a materialistic philosophy, or second, to confirm the materialism they had previously and hypothetically postulated as the nature of reality.

Materialistic mechanism is by no means to be considered a modern invention of thought. It is very old fashioned. The Greek philosopher Democritus deserves credit for having imagined, in the fifth century B.C., what an atom is.[4] Swimming against the mainstream of Platonic dualism and idealism, the materialists conceived of the tiniest particle of matter, which literally could not be cut or split. This irreducible "a-tom" was thought to be constitutive not only of visible objects that occupy space, but also of the invisible soul. Following Democritus four centuries later in Rome, Lucretius explained that atoms are "seeds exceedingly round and exceedingly minute," and virtually weightless. Therefore, even the soul "must consist of very small seeds and be inwoven through veins and flesh and sinews."[5]

Taking a long leap in time, we find that the seventeenth century stands out in the history of Western science as the time when scientists and philosophers became most fascinated by the analogy of the machine as the structure and mobile power of all matter.[6] Simple and crude as their machines actually were, they nevertheless suggested a similarity between mechanical contrivances and the workings of nature. Whether in animal life or human beings, or in the movements of winds and ocean tides or planets and stars, everything appeared to be mechanical. The great thinkers of that century and the next—Francis Bacon, Thomas Hobbes, Rene Descartes, G. W. Leibniz, and Immanuel Kant, among many others—all accepted the analogy, but with differences of intensity and world view. The mechanical model of reality could be materialistic *only*, in a monistic way—that is, not admitting of *anything* being immaterial. Or else, dualism could embrace mechanism as an explanation of the structure of all physical and organic things, but nevertheless insist on the need for the addition of an immaterial soul. To sort out all those thinkers and the shades of their theories is the task of a distinguished historian of science such as Stanley Jaki. What interests us here is the rise and spread of modern mechanistic materialism from that time.

Writing at the end of the seventeenth century, an English theologian complained:

But the Mechanic Philosophy that is lately come in vogue has set some men upon an Attempt to frame a Hypothesis about the Nature of the Soul. . . . It makes the Soul not to be anything really distinct from the Body: But only such a Disposition of the Parts of the Body, as makes it fit to live, move, remember, think, etc., all which they think may be done by a System of Matter, provided there be Skill enough in the Contriver; and they refer to the infinite Art of God.[7]

A generation later, the founder of Methodism was himself fascinated by the mechanical analogy to the human body. John Wesley said this in a sermon:

How fearfully and wonderfully wrought into innumerable fibres, nerves, membranes, muscles, arteries, veins, vessels of various kinds! And how amazingly is the dust connected with water, with inclosed [sic] circulating fluids, diversified a thousand ways by a thousand tubes and strainers. Yea, and how wonderfully is air impacted into every part, solid or fluid, of the animal machine. . . . But all this would not avail, were not ethereal fire intimately mixed with this earth, air, and water.[8]

The clear and categorical difference between these two comments on mechanism and the philosophy of the thoroughgoing materialists is like the distinction between a metaphor and a definitive statement. It is one thing to say that all organisms, entities, and substances are arranged and operate *like* machines. It is quite another to assert that they *are* machines, and are *only* machines. With respect to human beings, one can cautiously admit that the religious views of Catholic Descartes and Anglican Wesley are acceptable to nonmaterialists. They held dualistic concepts of life. For Descartes, the body-machine requires a soul from outside; for Wesley, an "ethereal fire," which probably meant the same as the soul. Immanuel Kant's inclination "to explain all products and events of nature . . . on mechanical lines"[9] nonetheless included the dimension of purpose, finality, and teleology. *That* was the vexed and debated issue during the nineteenth century, as the accelerating scientific research provided more and more data to confirm the theory of mechanists. Is there any purpose for natural, organic processes? Can reconciliation be reached between the claims of idealistic philosophy and materialistic philosophy, so that the metaphysical power of divine soul or spirit can be discerned even in the ongoing processes of mutation, natural selection of species, and especially human life? Darwin and Darwinism, with all their import for philosophy and theology, brought the new factor that compelled idealists and materialists, as well as Christian believers and agnostics, to take sides in the struggle to redefine humanity.[10]

Today we are still engaged in that struggle, but in greatly changed circumstances. It is no longer just a limited debate over creation and the evolving of *homo sapiens* from earlier primates or hominids.[11] More than a century after Darwin, little doubt exists that a mechanistic understanding of all living organisms prevails among scientists, psychologists, physicians, and philosophers, though with numerous exceptions, of course. In all likelihood a majority of them adhere to a materialistic, mechanistic world view as their *operational* theory, even if not consistently in personal living.

The other new aspect of our situation today is the scientific society, the technological culture, in which we all live. We must admittedly guard against making generalizations about the human race as such, and even about all Americans. But most of us live in the technological culture and take it for granted. We belong to it; we enjoy its innumerable benefits; and only the romanticists want to flee from it and live on organic farms or remote tropical islands. It would be unrealistic, dishonest, and ill mannered for me to denounce science-based technology altogether. Nevertheless, many of us share in the spreading social sense of anxiety over its pathological consequences.

Now we must look briefly and candidly at some evidences of this alleged pathology. We concede that the present state of our total scientific society has been attained to a large extent by persons holding the mechanistic world view. Can we show that the inevitable product of this view is an uninhibited and rapid growth of all-embracing technology that is at least as perilous to human well-being as it is promising? An immense amount of data would need to be placed on each pan of the huge scales that weigh the goods and promises of technology against the ills and perils. Perhaps even then a reading would be inconclusive, since we lack such objective instrumentation to measure what we call human values. So we shape our judgments largely by observation and educated intuition.*

From the wide spectrum of technical achievement in our lifetime, I would choose *four* recent developments for illustrative consideration. These four are genetic science, engineered reproduction, artificial organs, and computers.

GENETIC SCIENCE

The challenge of molecular biology to traditional humanistic and religious concepts of human life needs to be taken very seriously. Not only the nature of life, but its purpose and worth are called into question by the rapidly growing knowledge of DNA and cellular development. If the human organism can ostensibly be reduced to an assortment of proteins and amino acids, hardly distinguishable at molecular level from those of other organisms, where is the distinctiveness of human life to be found? And if found, how explained?

An explicitly materialistic, reductionist statement is made by the popular scientist Carl Sagan in his serious article in the *Encyclopaedia Britannica:* "Man is a tribute to the subtlety of matter."[12] This is his own profession of faith in matter, rather than a demonstrable thesis. But, if agreed to and accepted, it expresses the mechanistic notion that everything that constitutes the phenomenon of your body and mind is already present, latent and potential, in the chromosomes of the embryo. The source of that "subtlety," however, has yet to be discovered, though according to a consistent mechanistic theory continuing research may eventually reveal a source.[13]

---

*In passing, notice how our vernacular vocabulary reveals how our collective mentality gives expression to the mechanistic world view. We say that genes and reproduction are *engineered.* Genes and our minds are *programmed.* Brains are *wired;* or if that word is too gross and clumsy to be contemporary, our neurosensory systems are likened to electronic *microcircuitry* and *microchips,* rather than vice versa. We call DNA molecules *building blocks;* newly fertilized ova are *blueprints of life.* Pain and suffering are now *managed. Structure* has become a verb. And related to everything are *mechanisms* of thought. Do thoughts create vocabulary? Or does common vocabulary inevitably shape our thoughts?

From a mechanistic starting point, and with a deliberate concern only to find knowledge of how DNA works, genetic science inevitably acquires a moral character. The same materialist who claims to see human life only mechanistically becomes a party to providing benefits for human health and economics, preventing and curing diseases, reducing suffering, producing food. For these reasons, his research is warmly welcomed as an enhancer of life's goodness.

Such research, however, also contains certain risks. The promises of genetics ought not seduce people into believing that by a eugenic program human beings can be so controlled and manipulated as to become perfect specimens of physical form, intelligence, and health. The uses of recombinant DNA in agriculture may possibly have disruptive effects upon ecosystems of the natural environment, although this result has not been demonstrated as yet. The application of new procedures of gene therapy for human diseases of individual patients, soon to be tried, may be safer than allowing the disease to run its lethal course. However, even when newly spliced genes are directed to somatic cells in bone marrow, an indeterminate danger exists that congenital mutations may inadvertently be caused. That danger would be greatly expanded in the much debated procedure of changing germ-line cell nuclei in vitro, either for therapeutic purposes or for modifying physical traits in the individual eventually to be born.

ENGINEERED REPRODUCTION

Reproduction is another one of those words that mechanistic thinking has made current in our speech, instead of *procreation*. The acquiring of knowledge about the procreation of human beings is likewise rushing ahead of our capacity to reach informed positions on some inherent moral issues. The first person born after in vitro fertilization (IVF), Louise Joy Brown, is only seven years old; but there are already hundreds of other babies and children whose individual existence began in a glass.

No procedure affecting the very nature of human life can seem to be more mechanistic and materialistic than the technique of assisted reproduction. The in vitro technique requires the collaboration of experts in the exacting scientific disciplines of endocrinology, embryology, and gynecology. If the technique is so mechanical, does it require of its technicians a mechanistic philosophy of human life as well? No, not a requirement. The American pioneers of in vitro fertilization, Doctors Howard and Georgeanna Jones of Norfolk, Virginia, are certified Christians: not mechanists but Methodists! Their first protocol for IVF was consistent with theological insights concerning the nature and value of human life.[14] Nevertheless, the technique of IVF lends itself very conveniently to a philosophy of mechanistic materialism.

Consider, for example, a most thorough study of artificial aids to fertilization made at the behest of Her Majesty's Government by the Warnock Committee.[15] In its report of July 1984, the committee made recommendations for policy and legislation that would cover most of the possible techniques for engineering reproduction. These are artificial insemination, in vitro fertilization, ovum donation, "harvesting" (as they say) of embryos by lavage as with livestock, embryo freezing, ovum freezing, embryo research, hybridization, and surrogate motherhood. What seems clear from the report is the committee's assumption that many researchers and physicians would have no scruple about using organic tissue as though it were material for constructing a machine. Otherwise the report would not be so guarded about the uses of the embryo, and also so protective of the values of natural motherhood, fatherhood, and familial relations.

The report gives the initial judgment that infertility is a medical indication, not a regrettable inconvenience; it should therefore be treated by proper means under the National Health Service. No doubt, most researchers, physicians, and others who work to correct infertility do so with the right intention to assist the couple in having a baby. The Warnock report seems to fear, however, that some will disregard valued human factors in the process. Therefore, a licensing authority should be established by legislation of Parliament to oversee and regulate the whole range of possible procedures. Artificial insemination by both husband and so-called donor (vendor!) is approved but subject to hygienic and genetic conditions. IVF is also approved, including the use of frozen embryos (the most disputed point); but embryos may not be kept alive without being implanted for more than fourteen days, and none may be implanted if already used for research (another disputed point). The technique of embryo transfer by lavage—used extensively now with cattle—is prohibited, as is also "surrogacy," or the use of surrogate mothers.

As expected, the report has been severely criticized for being either too permissive or too restrictive, depending upon the views of the critics. But the report evidently manifests a sensitivity on the part of the committee members to the excesses to which a purely mechanistic view of life can lead.

ARTIFICIAL ORGANS (HEARTS)

To be more literal and accurate, the artificial heart would be called the cardiac machine. It is a machine, not a heart; plastic, not flesh. In what sense are current experiments justified? And do they exemplify a mechanistic materialism? Both questions are ambiguous and difficult to answer.

The inventors of cardiac machines, the surgeons and physicians who implant them, and the patients who desperately accept them, are all witnesses to the basic human desires to remain alive and to help others to live. The altruistic intent to devise a therapy for end-stage heart disease is as laudable as the creative intelligence needed to achieve it. Those few who have pioneered in this bold venture have already earned a place in medical history.

If one judges from the perspective of thousands of sufferers from advanced heart disease or defect who are unable to secure human heart transplants, the research and experimentation on cardiac machines seems to be not only justifiable but very urgent. That view is theoretical, commended as though it were just one more instance of medical research. However, from the first implanting of the Jarvik-7 in the thoracic cavity of Dr. Barney Clark in Utah to the present cases reported sensationally in the news media, many questions have been raised about the legitimacy of the whole enterprise.

One question may seem sentimental, but for many people it is a real one. It concerns the natural integrity of the human body. Is not the integrity of the whole person a given in creation? Already most remarkable procedures have been developed by plastic and prosthetic surgeons to replace faulty parts of flesh and bone with artificial ones of metal and plastic—joints for knees and hips, pacemakers to regulate the heartbeat, electronic implants to aid hearing—to say nothing of familiar old devices like artificial legs and gold teeth. Where does this stop, before we produce human cyborgs who increasingly approximate machines?

The heart possesses a virtually universal symbolism, a mystique, and commands a religious veneration about which many pages could be written. Such symbolism is not insignificant. Just try substituting *liver* or *pancreas* in our colloquial expressions about the heart. Could one lover say to the beloved, "Here is my liver"? Or think of John Wesley's famous conversion, if he had said, "My gallbladder was strangely warmed." In biblical terms, the ancient Hebrews perceived the fault of Greek dualism and asserted the unity of body and soul, of head and heart. Indeed, the Hebrew word *lebh* for heart designates not so much that great metronomic muscle in the chest as it means something like the reasoning mind of the whole person. So here is a common question: Does religious teaching forbid surgical invasion and transplants? No . . . not entirely. It seems clear, though, that the cardiac machine, as well as transplant surgery, is shattering the traditional nonmedical, romantic, religious meanings of *heart*.

Another and more important question about materialism and the experimentation with cardiac machines is threefold: it is social, economic, and political. The best-informed and most perceptive writer about artificial hearts is Dr. Lawrence K. Altman of the *New York Times*. He predicts, "It will take hundreds more Mr. Schroeders to determine if artificial hearts can overcome the hurdle of delivering a reasonable quality of life and find their way into standard medical practice."[16] The cardiac machine promises the forestalling of death—but only for the few, and only for a short time, unless a natural heart transplant can be achieved. All the publicity stimulated and orchestrated by the Humana Corporation, with slavish cooperation of the mass media, has upgraded the optimism and expectation of an ever more credulous public. And pressures remain on the federal government to continue financing the program in spite of much expert medical opinion to the contrary. All of which, I would submit, is reflective of a mechanistic view of the experimental subjects themselves and a materialistic perception of the economic profits to be garnered if, after colossal expense and human pain, the procedure can become routinized.

COMPUTERS

Thomas B. Sheridan, professor of mechanical engineering at MIT, lecturing on that campus in 1979, spoke of the four great "insults" to human self-confidence and sufficiency. These insults were and are the devastating effects of the achievements of four great scientists. First was Copernicus, whose unintended insult was to show that the realm of humanity "is not discontinuous from the rest of the physical universe." The second was Darwin, who demonstrated that humanity does not enjoy a clear discontinuity from animals. Freud was the third, because he argued that humans are not above and free from their carnal instincts and drives. Professor Norbert Wiener, founder of cybernetics, was the fourth, presenting us with the nervous question of "whether man is ultimately any more or better than a machine."[17] To those four insults a fifth should be added, I believe. That is linked to the names of Francis Crick and James Watson, who revealed the nature of the DNA molecule and thereby led to the questioning of human discontinuity from all living matter.

It is easy to say that computers are merely tools, and that they are designed to do only what women and men, and even children, tell them to do. If tools like scalpels and spades extend the work of the hands, then computers extend the work of the mind. So we are told. This consoling maxim applies aptly to a great number of ways computers are employed. And if we are at all content with life in our scientific society, we can be grateful for the computer's power to save us from confusion, error, and excessive working time. Imagine going back twenty years or so to the manner of agents' checking reservations on the worldwide airline networks by using telephone calls and manual typewriters; or returning to the adding machines and written notes used in accounting, banking, and big business. Today, as computer science and technical application keep running ahead of our information and understanding, and even ahead of our imagination, we can describe the progress in terms of mystification, amazement, and miracle. What confronts us now is not simply the word processor, or the calculator, or the automatic pilot on jet planes. Norbert Wiener's *Golem* is now giving us automated industries, robots in factories, and the diagnostic and supervisory competence of computers made to have artificial intelligence.

The neuralgic question, then, is not simply whether computers are the most prodigious and efficient of all tools invented by humankind. It is quite seriously the question of whether millions of human beings are destined to lose their sense of competitive competence, their jobs, and even their civil freedoms. These are the genuine problems that Professor Sheridan foresaw in 1979, and for which he offered general resolutions. In the same lecture series, however, his colleague the eminent computer scientist Joseph Weizenbaum was much more reluctant to suggest a solution to the inevitable increase in the computerization of our society and the decrease in human self-esteem and responsibility. Weizenbaum spoke, rather, in almost apocalyptic terms of the coming time when human beings accept one another as machines and as "merely symbol manipulators and information processors."[18] More optimistically, Sheridan believed that it is possible "to make evident and celebrate what people *are* that computers are *not*," and to educate people in ways to live in a computerized world without losing their humanity. But the details of that noble and awesome task remain undefined.

Again and again we hear of the depersonalizing effects of computerized technology. The allegations may or may not be exaggerated. Whatever their truth, we are asking here whether the many pressures exerted upon human beings to conform to machines are the consequence of the mechanistic mentality expressing itself in invention, development, production, and deployment of computerized machines. Certainly, the computer is the most fitting analogy or example of what the mechanistic human looks like according to a materialistic conception.

DUALISTIC DANGERS

Turning from mechanism, let us look in a briefer manner at dualism. What is dualism? How is it related to science, technology, and human life? And how in the world can such a complicated concept be called dangerous?

Prior to dualism are numerous obvious dualities. We humans inevitably perceive the dualities of nature and include these perceptions in our normal thought patterns and speech. The most obvious dualities are light and dark, day and night, heat and cold. Some of the dualities are in opposition, such as good and evil, life and death. Others are complementary, such as male and female, left brain and right brain, subject and object, memory and hope. But philosophers and psychologists argue with some passion over the question of complementarity of these dual entities, or especially about the relation of mind and body, or mind and brain.[19]

The ancient Chinese saw all of reality to consist of the relatedness of parts of the cosmic duality called yang and yin. Indian philosophy is dualistic, but sees the ultimate reconciling of divided dualities as the coincidence of opposites. In Christianity, the central doctrine of Incarnation and the person of Jesus Christ asserts the uniting of the fully divine nature with the fully human nature in the one person of Christ, thus overcoming the ultimate duality of creator and creature, of body and soul, and of finite and infinite. Although this theological doctrine of Incarnation may appear to be utterly remote from modern science, it is a clue to understanding the nature of human life in a *non*dualistic, unitary way. By this I mean the concept of a person that does not keep body and soul or spirit divided, and that does not allow the integral unity of body and soul to collapse into either materialism of the body, on one side, or spiritualism of the soul on the other.

Throughout history, from the Greek philosophy of Plato and ancient Hinduism, there have been extremely compelling dispositions to think of human life dualistically.[20] Human life consists of finite body and immortal soul in a disjunctive relationship. But the body and soul, matter and spirit are in an unstable relation, according to this kind of dualism. This kind of dualism maximizes the estimate of value of the soul to the point where the physical body is of minimal importance. The body is seen as inert and passive unless it receives an infusion of the soul from an external source, such as God, Brahma, or the eternal oversoul.

The classic illustration of such unstable dualism was painted by Michelangelo in his famous Sistine Chapel fresco of "The Creation of Adam."[21] We can all visualize it. Here is the body of Adam in heroic proportions, like Mr. Universe or iron-pumper Arnold Schwarzenegger. There is the finger of a heavenly grandfather God, the finger of creation, stuck forward vigorously to impart the divine power of life to Adam's lax and recumbent body.

Michelangelo was schooled in the reborn, dualistic Platonism of fifteenth-century Renaissance Florence. His God is an Olympian figure from Greek mythology, rather than the Creator God of the Bible. His Adam is a heroic demigod, like Hercules, rather than the Bible's authentic man who unites body and soul into one integrated person: the psychosomatic person.

This is exactly how numerous people think of human life today. So far as their dualism is concerned, it seems not to matter whether they are believers or agnostics. Contrary to biblical anthropology, they reduce the essence and meaning of life to pure spirit and spirituality. This is just as wrong in relation to the biblical insight as is its opposite, namely, the reduction of all life to "the subtlety of matter."

Such words as *spirituality* and *spiritual values* are generally respected and honored both within and apart from religious communities. How can it be charged, then, that a one-sided spiritualizing of human life is dangerous in a scientific society? If people believe that matter does not matter, that only the soul or spirit matters, what are the practical consequences for their attitude toward science? Four implications can be noted and (I would add) deplored.

1. Exclusive preoccupation with the soul or spirit inclines one to an indifference to scientific progress. It fosters a

rejection of technology as such, and a desire to escape to an otherworldly realm of experience.

2. It may also involve the pursuit and embracing of esoteric religious cults that promise arcane, occult knowledge. This may mean renunciation of the world for a Sufi, Hindu, or Buddhist in favor of mystical experience; or it may be expressed in extreme forms of Christian apocalypticism.

3. In consequence, therefore, the very spiritualized concept of human life may mean a lack of a sense of moral responsibility for social injustice and the well-being of all persons in society.

4. Very ironically, unbalanced dualism often leads people to disdain care and concern for the body in a manner more usually attributed to materialism, which is the opposite of spiritualism. This can take the form of deliberate abuse of the body as well as the trivializing of death. If only the spirit or soul matters, then it is unimportant what happens to the body. Sensuality, alcoholism, and drug addiction are allowed to reign, while medical treatment and surgical procedures are rejected and denied. Euthanasia and suicide are easily justified. In these respects, the spiritualist and the materialist join hands in a strange uniting of opposites.

It is neither scientifically nor intellectually acceptable to press the overt consequences of both materialistic mechanism and dualism too far. Many exceptions exist to the four phenomena just mentioned, because the factors that determine behavior are as complex as all human experiences. Yet, a searching and critical examination of the effects of these two opposing philosophies or world views upon our efforts to enhance a good human life is urgently needed. Neither of them can serve as the criterion for science. But the view and understanding of human life that is derived from the Hebrew and Christian Scriptures and developed in both ancient and contemporary thought does serve that normative purpose. Neither materialistic nor idealized nor spiritualized, this is the integrated life of human wholeness: the functioning unity of soul and body.

PANEL DISCUSSION

LURIA: Dr. Nelson was certainly extremely eloquent; he went as far as it is possible to try to convert me from a monistic materialist to something that he advocates. I regret to say he didn't quite succeed in that task, but he made many other interesting, suggestive, and provocative points.

While I was listening to him I was comparing the situation into which technology puts modern society to the plight of the Jews in Babylon, and comparing two books of the Bible in that connection: the books of Jeremiah and of Ezra. Jeremiah complained and lamented and warned about the possible problems that were going to happen, where Ezra was really nothing but a political organizer—took the Jews out and brought them back to Israel, to Palestine, after having made a deal with the new king of Persia.

That is really a thought worth considering. You may warn as much as you can about the possible dangers of a situation concerning technology or anything else, but what you have to do is to organize to get the changes you want, because all of the lamenting and the warning accomplishes very little.

KEVLES: I'd like to add to what Professor Luria has said, perhaps in a way that's a little more pointed. With regard to Dr. Nelson's critique of (and in ways attack on) mechanistic materialism in genetic science and reproductive technologies, I think he is fighting a magnificent rearguard action. One of the basic points he makes so eloquently is that we are increasingly confronted with a menu of technological options in genetics and reproduction that, in a sense, take us away from our traditional and indeed ancient notions of humanity.

My mind reaches back, as a historian's mind is wont to do, to attitudes concerning contraception, abortion, and even artificial insemination by donor (AID) over the last century. The technology of contraception was extremely controversial and was attacked from various quarters at the end of the nineteenth and through the first half of the twentieth century (and even beyond that, in certain states) as demeaning to ourselves as human beings, as denying true, full womanhood, as reducing us to

animals because it permitted sexual gratification without reproductive consequences. Well, we know what happened to those
attitudes concerning contraception, even though there are minor rearguard actions concerning them being fought now—
with which I do not want to associate Dr. Nelson.

Attitudes toward abortion present a similar case. To be sure,
abortion has not achieved the same widespread acceptance in
our society as contraception has. Nevertheless, compared to the
hostile, virulent opposition to abortion, which was embraced,
believe it or not, even by eugenicists as late as the 1930s, the
degree of change in opinion toward that is truly astonishing. As
late as the 1950s, artificial insemination by donor was regarded
as anathema in many quarters, and most people just simply
wouldn't partake of it. But attitudes toward that have changed
sharply in the last ten or fifteen years.

If we look back over these changes and try to apply some sort
of rule or inference arising from them, what will count in the
end (whether we like it or not) is not some abstract notion of
whether these things are truly human or humane or express or
counter human values, but whether these innovations serve the
self-interest of the complete human being or some large group
of human beings in ways that they find satisfying. If people
want children and can't have them in a normal, traditional way,
then they will resort to IVF, they will resort to AID, they will
resort to surrogate motherhood, and so on.

So I think, with regard to these new technologies that are
coming, whether we like it or not, the same kind of rule of self-
interest will be applied. Human values tend to express those
things. I think Dr. Nelson is fighting a rearguard action. I think
also that this is a rearguard action that *must* be fought because
what we have to do is reinterpret continually what human values
will mean to us as measured against and in the context of the
realities of technological possibility.

NELSON: Well, it's very deflating because I thought I was in the
vanguard; now I'm in the rearguard. At least from some perspectives, I am in the vanguard because a good many people
aren't even fighting any action in this area. But it may well be
as you said, in terms of the movement of reproductive technology; already things have gone so far in the directions we've
described that any criticisms seem to be somewhat passé.

I can't quite believe that and I don't think the popular acceptance is quite so universal as has been indicated. Otherwise,
why are people in so many dimensions of society still so very
agitated over the question of surrogate motherhood, or the
abortion question, which are very complex and have not totally
been accepted?

So, rather than being vanguard or rearguard (to use those
figures), I feel I am more involved in the middle of things as
we all move to adjust our thinking and also to apply our moral
perceptions to what is happening. Otherwise, I think we capit-
ulate to a kind of inevitable determinism—"what will be, will
be"—that what scientific engineering leads to is going to happen whether we can do anything about it or not. People still are
apprehensive about Aldous Huxley's New World, when babies
are decanted out of artificial wombs and relegated to differing
social statuses where some are drones and workers and others
are elite and so on.

Now, I don't want to beat that particular horse too much
because there's already been enough of that laceration, but even
so I think the prospects that once seemed totally fantastic and
unrealistic, as in Aldous Huxley's fantasy, have started to become real. And if we are content to let them go on that way, I
think scientifically, the artificial placenta might be developed.
But I do feel (maybe just intuitively, but also because of my
inevitable grounding in Christian faith and morality) that there
is an integrity about not only human persons as such, but human relationships and familial relationships, that is indispen-
sable to a good human life, so must somehow be preserved.

KEVLES: I want to advance a clarification. A sharp line must
be drawn and kept in mind between the demonic vision of *Brave
New World* and things that are here and now and possibly to
come. The sharp line is this: there is an enormous difference
between what people are willing to do for themselves, voluntarily, in consultation with medical authority, and what they are
compelled to do by the state or by some other coercive organization. I would agree with you emphatically, that one of the
worst things, perhaps *the* worst thing we could entertain and
advance, is to vest in the state the power to control our own
reproductive and genetic lives.

That has not happened so far, by and large. What we have in

cases of artificial insemination by donor, or contraception, or surrogate motherhood, or IVF, is a willing and voluntary participation by prospective parents in a particular kind of medical and reproductive technology.

The state is trying to interfere with some of this. Clearly, the abortion issue is an explosive and volatile one in which the state has become involved. I rather deplore the way the state has become involved in certain regards. That is perhaps the subject for another conference. I just want to make sure, though, that we keep in mind the difference between what is done voluntarily and what is done coercively.

NELSON: Another observation about artificial insemination. There are a good many sperm banks in the country now, I understand. They are no longer a laughing matter. You used to talk about making your deposit in the First National Sperm Bank and so on, but that's no longer a joking matter; and yet unless I'm uninformed, or ill-informed, there are no publicly accepted standards of regulation over these sperm banks. They are a matter of free enterprise and are uncontrolled and subject to the skill or the sense of responsibility of the people who run them. At least it was so until very recently.

Another thing about artificial insemination is a matter of a scientific survey among physicians who use the method and found (about six years ago, anyway) that at least 80 percent of those physicians had only minimal knowledge of genetics. They had not bothered at all to try to trace the history of the usual medical students who sell their sperm for that purpose. They had no idea as to how many offspring there were in a given community from the same lender or donor. In other words, it was without regulation and very haphazard.

Now one could say that in a good rational society all those matters will be ordered and rationalized according to some kind of health measures which a board of health or federal agency might impose. But for the present time, that is not the case. I think this is why the Warnock Committee in Great Britain startled the American perspective, at least, by saying that there should be a licensing board established by the British government to oversee all of these kinds of procedures affecting reproduction. That would not fly very well in this country, but nevertheless there is thinking about it.

BYRNE: If a human being can make significant moral choices, need it matter so much as to how the human being is ontologically constituted? In other words, must materialism presuppose determinism?

NELSON: I don't think materialism presupposes determinism, unless one assumes at the same time there is inherently in matter something that is determined. On the contrary, I think the more likely view on the effects of materialism would be that everything is random. The famous phrase "chance of necessity" is really an emphasis upon the chance, the randomness of happenings. Now, there are, of course, those who have participated in Nobel Conferences in past years, like E. O. Wilson and other advocates of genetic determinism. That may be what is in the mind of the questioner. If genetics or organic material with genes is seen to be the bearer of inexorable deterministic consequences on human life and consciousness, and even on conscious and moral behavior, then that is a kind of determinism, to be sure. That is a very much disputed issue, and I certainly do not subscribe to it.

KEVLES: I just wanted to respond to the question simply because we know that we are in some sense programmed to become what we are by the information coded in our genome. Let us remember that the information, in order to be coded and operative, requires an environment in which it must become operative. We are not the product simply of genes. We are the product of the combination of genes and environment, and the varieties of environment are infinite in which this genome might develop. It doesn't seem to me that distinctiveness of ourselves as human beings falls away with the reduction, knowing that we are somehow the product of genome and the environment in which it develops. We are more than just genes. We are more than just a handful of chemicals. We are a very complicated system of interactive parts. Nobody knows how it all works, and there is plenty of room left for spirit, free will, and so on, in my opinion.

NOTES

1. The fact of pervasive technology is too obvious to warrant documenting; but interpretations of its significance for humanity and nonhuman nature

are very diverse. They run from uncritical optimism to critical optimism to hypercritical pessimism. See J. Robert Nelson, *Science and Our Troubled Conscience* (Philadelphia: Fortress Press, 1980), 15–23.

2. At Nobel Conference IV, 1968, W. H. Thorpe discussed the materialistic presupposition, which is accepted by numerous scientists: "Vitalism and Organicism," in *The Uniqueness of Man,* ed. John D. Roslansky (Amsterdam: North Holland, 1969), 74.

3. Richard Levins and Richard Lewontin, *The Dialectical Biologists* (Cambridge: Harvard University Press, 1985).

4. Bertrand Russell, *History of Western Philosophy* (London: George Allen and Unwin, Ltd., 1946), 85–92.

5. Lucretius, "On the Nature of Things," in *Great Books of the Western World,* vol. 12 (Chicago: Encyclopaedia Britannica, 1952), 26.

6. Stanley L. Jaki, *The Road of Science and the Ways of God* (Chicago: University of Chicago Press, 1978), 50–79.

7. W. Wall, *Baptism* (London: Richard Burroughs, 1707), 129.

8. John Wesley, *Works,* vol. 6 (1872; reprint, Grand Rapids: Zondervan, n.d.), 219.

9. Immanuel Kant, *The Critique of Teleological Judgment,* in *Great Books of the Western World,* vol. 42, 567.

10. *Darwin's Legacy,* Nobel Conference XVIII, 1982, ed. Charles L. Hamrum (San Francisco: Harper & Row, 1983).

11. Conrad Hyers, *The Meaning of Creation* (Atlanta: John Knox Press, 1984); *The Origins of Life,* trans. Peter Heinegg (San Francisco: Harper & Row, 1982).

12. *Encyclopaedia Britannica,* 15th ed., Macropaedia, s.v. "life."

13. Sir Francis Crick declared, "All life is reducible to chemistry and physics. That is the certainty on which biology is founded." Cited in a lecture by Everett Mendelsohn.

14. The protocols for in vitro fertilization as written by the Drs. Jones at the Norfolk, Virginia, clinic were extremely circumspect about respecting the human embryo as well as the value of parenthood. See J. Robert Nelson, *Troubled Conscience,* 136–37.

15. *Report of the Committee of Inquiry into Human Fertilisation and Embryology,* chairman, Dame Mary Warnock, DBE (London: Her Majesty's Stationery Office, July 1984).

16. Lawrence K. Altman, M.D., *New York Times,* 8 April 1985, 9.

17. Thomas B. Sheridan, "Computer Control and Human Alienation," in *Faith and Science in an Unjust World,* ed. Roger L. Shinn (Philadelphia: Fortress Press, 1980), 300. See also Norbert Wiener, *God and Golem, Inc.* (Cambridge: MIT Press, 1964).

18. Joseph Weizenbaum, "Technological Detoxification," in *Faith and Science in an Unjust World,* 305.

19. John C. Eccles, "The Experiencing Self," in *The Uniqueness of Man,* 103–35. Max Delbruck, "Mind from Matter?" in *The Nature of Life,* Nobel Conference XIII, 1977, ed. William H. Heidcamp (Baltimore: University Park Press, 1978), 141–69.

20. J. Robert Nelson, *Human Life* (Philadelphia: Fortress Press, 1984), 36–43, 59–65.

21. Ibid., 66–68.

General Panel Discussion: Responsible Science

BYRNE: Professor Luria, is not the ignorance of, or the ignoring of, the second law of thermodynamics by technologists and some scientists the major cause of problems in the environment?

LURIA: I don't quite understand what the question may mean, because ignoring the second law of thermodynamics is like ignoring gravity when you go out for a walk!

What is might mean is this. Some people have warned that the second law of thermodynamics—by which every set of reactions in certain conditions tends to get down to equilibrium and therefore to mechanical debt, in the sense that no more energy is available—may be also the fate of life. This is a complete misunderstanding, because it's exactly the opposite that happens. Let's call it the invention of life (whether life was created or created itself by evolution). The apparent invention of life was exactly to find a way to escape, in a very small part of the universe and on a very small part of the matter on earth, that tendency to decay that ultimately brings about everything freezing without energy. Life takes energy away from other parts of the environment to put it into the order and the organization of a living organism. It doesn't contradict the second law of thermodynamics; it simply bypasses it.

BYRNE: Dr. Brill, you spoke about high school students carrying out experiments in genetic engineering. What kinds of controls are placed on such studies, if any?

BRILL: High school seems to have slipped between the cracks. The controls up to now have generally been voluntary. There have been some guidelines that have evolved with experience. With experience, almost everybody in the technology has realized that the worst fears have disappeared. There is no real concern about most of the genetic engineering experiments that are going on, and the ones that are going on in high schools, I assume, are very simple experiments where one could take a known gene and put it into a known bacterium. Just repeating something that has been done thousands and thousands of times in many laboratories with no problems and no expected problems.

As I said in my talk, regulatory agencies are now looking into the possible dangers that might come out of biotechnology. They are talking with scientists and concerned citizens. Politicians are involved, of course, and so on. This is a very interesting time now because over the next year, I believe, there will be some regulations that we all will have to abide by. Right now there are no regulations for industry and there are no regulations for high school students. I have not heard a concern whatsoever about high schools.

BYRNE: Dr. Smith, do you believe that the counterculture of the 1960s and 1970s represented an attempt to return to the spiritual values of Jefferson's view of progress?

SMITH: I think to a degree that is true. I know more about the counterculture of the 1840s and 1850s than I do about the counterculture of the 1960s and 1970s. But if there is an analogy to be drawn there, it is that during the 1840s when we began to see the rise of various transcendentalist communities—utopian experiments, utopian socialism, whatever you want to call it—many of them were a direct response to the problems created by the rise of an industrial civilization. There is no doubt about that. Much of the philosophy that lay behind those communities was Jeffersonian in nature, in the sense that the emphasis was on trying to live a full life and yet to be productive.

A good example would be the Oneida Community, which was located in upstate New York and was the producer of the famous Oneida silver plate. That was a utopian socialist community. It operated under the principles of what was called Christian socialism, and it had a number of unusual practices, such as complex marriage, which people in the locality objected to because it had to do with some eugenic selection. In the long run this community disappeared, as did most of these utopian communities.

They stood for the principles of Jeffersonianism in that they supported an attempt to bring the spiritual and the material needs of life into better balance. I would think that in a way the counterculture of the sixties and seventies attempted to do the same thing. It is too early to tell. Many of these communities still exist in California and other places. They are still thriving. Whether they meet the same fate as the so-called counterculture of the 1840s and 1850s remains to be seen.

BYRNE: Dan Kevles, from California.

KEVLES: Living in California I can tell you there is no such thing as the counterculture in any uniform sense, and that must be kept in mind. Part of the counterculture was utopian: back-to-the-land romanticism, flight from the urban megalopolis, and from an environment of pollution and degradation, and so on. But there was also a very vigorous part of the counterculture that was no such thing, except perhaps rhetorically. It consisted of a self-indulgence in the benefits of technology; for example, the contraceptive pill, stereos, television, audio amplifiers, and so on. At the same time there was also a kind of psychedelic, antirational and antiscientific theme to it that was extremely strong. You could not help but notice it if you went to certain parts of Los Angeles, or the San Francisco Peninsula, and above all if you visited Berkeley, which I did a number of times in those years. That part of the counterculture Jefferson would have found appalling, utterly appalling.

BYRNE: Dr. Brill, most of your comments on biotechnology have pointed toward producing more grain and livestock products, which is causing overproduction in agriculture. Why not have our land-grant universities and large chemical companies concentrate more on new byproducts from grain and livestock, which would help solve our farmers' financial problems and really make an impact on society?

BRILL: That's an important question. There are two parts to it. Number one is why the effort to produce more when we have excess already? I think most people will predict that this excess is temporary and bad weather conditions in other countries could change things dramatically.

The other point, which is the main part of the question, is what can we do with agriculture to keep agriculture going? What can we do to change the products? I'll give you a couple of examples. Researchers are taking waste products of a corn harvest and using biological techniques to convert them into energy substances, such as ethanol and methane. These activities are going on in a number of laboratories in both industry and land-grant universities. Another activity that has certainly been talked about a lot is producing insulin in a crop, having the plant make insulin or some other valuable product, then harvesting the crop, purifying insulin in that way. In other words, instead of the fermenter doing it, have the farmer make the product. The economics of that idea doesn't look good at this point, but it can change. People are reconsidering that all the time.

Those are just a few examples of many ideas people are toying with. Some of those are being worked on now and certainly will be worked on in the future, hopefully to help the farmer.

BYRNE: Dr. Kevles, if humankind's most precious possession is not the germ plasm, what is?

KEVLES: I don't know what it is but I do not think it is the germ plasm in the sense that eugenicists meant it. They glorified the germ plasm in that all other considerations must give way before it: considerations of dignity; members of diverse groups, especially those different from the majority; the notion of civil liberty; the notion of human value as it might be defined by how well you do on I.Q. tests given at that time. In that sense their explanations of the germ plasm above those considerations and many others certainly disqualifies the germ plasm as the most precious element. I don't know what it is, but I think that as human beings, we recognize a diversity in the things that we value—involving human relationships, dignity, love, truth. We see often many people who are very valuable and certainly have a high degree of self-worth who do not contribute their germ plasm or do not ensure that their germ plasm makes its way into the next generation. Clearly they do not think that the most important thing is the germ plasm. I don't know what it is, but it isn't that, in the sense that eugenicists said it was.

NELSON: I think virtually all human beings who are reflective on the issue would say that the most important thing about their lives is the germ plasm that brought them into existence. Because without it they simply would not exist. Whether they pass that on through procreation is still another matter.

However, I also caught the phrase in Dr. Kevles's lecture and wondered about it a bit, whether this really applies in individual cases to the desire for the continuity of lineage through one's germ plasm mated with that of one's spouse. That is a question that tends to get overlooked a great deal in all this discussion about reproductive engineering and technology; that it does not matter which sperm or ovum from what source produces the baby that happens to become the member of your family. Some would increasingly say it really doesn't matter very much. What they want to have is a baby and it has got to more or less look like their type of human being. That is enough.

And yet, I think this is a real problem in artificial insemination. There are good reports that many persons born as a result of artificial insemination, and not told about it, later on learn that they did not have a natural father as the acknowledged father in the family, and so they begin to wonder where they came from. Some reports I've read have shown some quite psychopathic responses to that kind of unanswered question. Who am I? Where do I come from? The same might be said in these other aspects of reproduction. Is it an important factor or not, to know that you have a family lineage?

Of course, you can immediately ask, What about adopted children? They are beloved just like other children, which is true. In fact, it is often said that one can say to an adopted child, you are loved even more than a natural child would be because you have been chosen, or you have been bought with a price, to use an ambiguous, biblical term.

BYRNE: Dr. Brill, is there not a problem in that the enhanced expression of one gene will in all likelihood affect the expression of other genes? In humans, for example, expression of human growth hormone causes deformity and early death.

BRILL: I think that is the biggest challenge for the genetic engineer, at least for somebody who wants genetically to engineer an animal or plant. By putting in a random gene, the greatest chance is you are going to weaken the animal or plant. Obviously, if you want something to survive a season in the field you are going to have to put in a gene that does not weaken the plant that much. That is really going to be the sophistication of the genetic engineering. It is, in fact, the other side of my argument why it is going to be impossible to make a plant into a weed. By simply putting a gene into a plant the probability will be either that the plant does not like the gene and will have to be babied quite a bit by us in order to survive, or it will not survive. The chances of it becoming a weed and taking over are extremely low.

BYRNE: Professor Luria, you mentioned the responsibility of government to science, but how can a democracy go about getting a responsible environment? It seems almost as impossible as changing human nature.

LURIA: Well, that's a very important question. I will rephrase it. The question is, How should the government in a well-ordered society respond to the needs for the constructive application of science? Certainly, a government can and does encourage the process of science in certain directions by giving funds or withholding funds according to the wisdom of elected officials. I was trying to suggest that it is very important that the citizens who elect the government, and the members of the government who are elected be very knowledgeable and clear, not only about the meaning of science, but also about the interaction between science and technology, without confusing it. It is perfectly possible for government, if the people so wish, to interfere with certain technologies without necessarily interfering with science. In the same way, it is possible for the government to prohibit the distribution or the taking into airplanes of bombs or explosives without inhibiting research in chemistry on potential explosive substances. The important thing is the awareness. One of the problems I was trying to suggest is that in our own society, even though it is probably one of the most democratic and well organized in the world, the greatest power over the uses of technology comes not from the people or the elected officials of government, but from the great corporations and from the military corporation association, which run most of our industrial technology. A government more aware and more responsible to what may be the real and openly expressed opinion of a large majority of people would be a better thing to strive for in controlling technology, rather than simply bemoaning what is happening.